free *indeed*

AWAKENING
to the
LIGHT *of* LIBERTY

For My Children

*Awake, sleeper,
and arise from the dead...*

free *indeed*

BRYAN DAVIS

Free Indeed

Copyright © 2018 by Bryan Davis

Published by Scrub Jay Journeys
P. O. Box 512
Middleton, TN 38052
www.scrubjayjourneys.com
email: info@scrubjayjourneys.com

All rights reserved. No part of this publication may be reproduced, distributed, or transmitted in any form or by any means, including photocopying, recording, or other electronic or mechanical methods, without the prior written permission of the publisher, except in the case of brief quotations embodied in critical reviews and certain other noncommercial uses permitted by copyright law.

ISBN Print: 978-1-946253-27-9
ISBN Epub: 978-1-946253-26-2
ISBN Mobi: 978-1-946253-25-5

First Printing – October 2018

Cover Design by Olivia Hofer/Cranford Design

Printed in the U.S.A.

Library of Congress Control Number: 2018909968

CHAPTER 1

Doomed to Struggle?

Are Christians enslaved to sin? Are they doomed to continue sinning while alive on earth?

These are not trivial questions.

Many professing Christians state that they are not enslaved to sin and that they don't want to sin, yet they go on to proclaim that they will continue sinning as long as they live.

Yet, perpetually doing something that you don't want to do is practically the definition of slavery. Being doomed to constant struggle is a slavish life. If a person is in a constant battle between his inner longings and the will of God, then he is in spiritual chains. If a person doesn't live up to the model that God has placed before him, which is Christ himself, and he grieves over his lack of ability to follow in Christ's footsteps, then he is truly a slave of sin, not of Christ.

The biblical model of a true Christian is different. There is no battle between what he wants to do and the desires of his master, because they are in harmony. He wants only his master's will. This is his yearning, a single-minded passion that the Apostle Paul describes:

> I have been crucified with Christ; and it is no longer I who live, but Christ lives in me; and the

life which I now live in the flesh I live by faith in the Son of God, who loved me, and delivered Himself up for me. (Galatians 2:20 NASB)

Christ is our life. The person we were before we became Christians is dead, gone, eliminated. As Paul teaches again:

Knowing this, that our old self was crucified with Him, that our body of sin might be done away with, that we should no longer be slaves to sin; for he who has died is freed from sin. (Romans 6:6-7 NASB)

The old self is the nature that tends to serve self, the flesh. Without the indwelling Holy Spirit, we tend to be self-indulgent, the passions in our lives being set to please our physical bodies, our instinctive obsessions, and our sensual pleasures. When Jesus comes in the power of his spirit, he destroys that sinful self. Paul again:

Now those who belong to Christ Jesus have crucified the flesh with its passions and desires. (Galatians 5:24 NASB)

And not only is that flesh dead, it is removed, taken away from its former status as the controlling factor in our lives.

And in Him you were also circumcised with a circumcision made without hands, in the removal of the body of the flesh by the circumcision of Christ. (Colossians 2:11 NASB)

Here we complete our thesis, that God, in his infinite love and wisdom, has provided for his followers by giving them the ability to obey. He has crucified the power that held them captive, and he has transformed them into people who walk as Christ walked. As Paul says:

> Therefore we have been buried with Him through baptism into death, in order that as Christ was raised from the dead through the glory of the Father, so we too might walk in newness of life. (Romans 6:4 NASB)

And again,

> For the death that He died, He died to sin, once for all; but the life that He lives, He lives to God. Even so consider yourselves to be dead to sin, but alive to God in Christ Jesus. (Romans 6:10-11 NASB)

This newness of life, this freedom from sin, is what brings us salvation. God makes us holy. He makes us fit to enter into his presence.

> But now having been freed from sin and enslaved to God, you derive your benefit, resulting in sanctification, and the outcome, eternal life. (Romans 6:22 NASB)

Has this truth—this life-giving, soul-saving truth—been lost in this generation of spiritual bondage? Are believers trapped in a dungeon of darkness, asleep in a foggy wasteland, unable to awaken to freedom?

The answer is an emphatic No. There is freedom,

real freedom, a freedom that truly breaks the bondage to sin. And it is available to all.

Yet, what is our response to this message of liberty? Do we take offense that such freedom is suggested, that someone has found the sinless life so obviously taught in the Scriptures?

And why might there be offense? Why do some who name the name of Christ have so much trouble believing that God has the power to truly set them free from sin? Why do they believe that they cannot possess the passion that should set them apart from the world? Why can they not reach out and take the most awesome gift that mankind can possibly receive?

Tragically, the church itself stands in the way. The words of our corrupted culture have influenced the church, giving it a low view of a Christian's true nature. In fact, this perception is so widespread that any contradictory stance is often dismissed as heretical, no matter what proof is provided in the Scriptures.

In each chapter, we will look at teachings of the church that have done great damage to those who follow them. Often they are catch phrases, quoted like bumper-sticker slogans that need no proof. They are logical fallacies, poorly constructed thoughts that float about without challenge, because those who chant them have no desire to delve into their gaping cracks and crevices. Some are even blasphemies, statements that impugn the very character of God and his Holy Spirit.

As we expose the myths and unravel the tangled words, we will reveal the evil core, the source of bondage that blinds and incapacitates professing believers.

The source is The Liar—Satan—the one who encourages Christians to be comfortable in a never-ending cycle of sin and ineffective repentance.

Let us end that cycle here and now. Let us expose the lies that have deceived countless believers, rooted them in hopeless futility, and lulled them to sleep in a vast wasteland of fruitless Christianity.

We must shine a light, awaken the sleepers, and set them free from barren soils. We can show the world the way to true life by demonstrating how to walk in step with the master every day without fail. We have the answer they are seeking, a life that is free indeed.

> Jesus answered them, "Truly, truly, I say to you, everyone who commits sin is the slave of sin. And the slave does not remain in the house forever; the son does remain forever. If therefore the Son shall make you free, you shall be free indeed." (John 8:34-36 NASB)

CHAPTER 2

Self Disease - My Will be Done

Why do so many professing Christians fail to live free from sin? The answer is what I call Self Disease. This malady is pervasive, a contagion spread throughout mankind that unleashes the most horrible symptoms the world can imagine. This disease spills murder into streets and family homes, it incites rape in back alleys and bedrooms, and it fosters incest, child abuse, robbery, divorce, terrorism, greed, malice, and every other kind of sin that has ever spoiled God's created landscape.

Although the disease is made manifest in varying degrees, nearly everyone who has ever lived has at one time suffered from it, and most victims display its evil symptoms throughout their lives, controlling it by various temporary measures. Only a few ever find the cure.

Self Disease is really the age-old problem of self-centeredness, the innate tendency toward fulfilling the desires of the flesh. We are born with one mantra, "My Will be Done!" From the time we sprang from the womb, screaming for warmth and nourishment, we began answering the fleshly call, appeasing every whim of the body, every yearning for comfort, whether from hunger, thirst, insecurity, or pain. That's all we knew. Self was our only input.

At this early time in our lives, such desire to please self wasn't sinful, because we had no capacity to understand God and his law. Yet, such self-orientation later became the root of sin when we decided to choose self instead of God, and that's when sin became our master.

Myriad remedies have been suggested to control inner passions—meditation and monasteries, sports and spas, and even valium and vodka—yet none has ever given complete freedom from slavery to selfish desires. Many have despaired of ever finding a cure, throwing their collective hands up in surrender, crying out that a remedy doesn't exist—not in drugs, sports, or even religion. If God cannot rout this disease, who can?

God does have a cure, but throughout history it has frequently been misapplied. The path to God's remedy began with the Mosaic Law, a system of order etched in stone, a set of laws and principles by which we were to govern our society and ourselves. And the Law was good. Its principles were sound. As the Apostle Paul said, "So then, the Law is holy, and the commandment is holy and righteous and good." (Romans 7:12 NASB) The man who could live by God's law would certainly find life and peace, as Moses said:

> And you shall again obey the LORD, and observe all His commandments which I command you today. Then the LORD your God will prosper you abundantly in all the work of your hand, in the offspring of your body and in

> the offspring of your cattle and in the produce of your ground, for the Lord will again rejoice over you for good, just as He rejoiced over your fathers; if you obey the Lord your God to keep His commandments and His statutes which are written in this book of the law, if you turn to the LORD your God with all your heart and soul. (Deuteronomy 30:8-10 NASB)

And contrary to popular opinion, this law was not too difficult to obey. In fact, Moses claimed that following it wholeheartedly was within reach.

> For this commandment which I command you today is not too difficult for you, nor is it out of reach. It is not in heaven, that you should say, "Who will go up to heaven for us to get it for us and make us hear it, that we may observe it?" Nor is it beyond the sea, that you should say, "Who will cross the sea for us to get it for us and make us hear it, that we may observe it?" But the word is very near you, in your mouth and in your heart, that you may observe it. (Deuteronomy 30:11-14 NASB)

The Law served as a guide toward abundant life, and, correctly followed, was a gateway to both spiritual and physical fulfillment for its adherents. Yet, it did not work. For centuries, millions of people, from devoted Jews to nominal Christians, have ascribed to the goodness of the Law, but they have not succeeded in obeying its calling. What happened? What was wrong with the Law?

According to Paul, our failure to obey was not the fault of the Mosaic Law.

> What shall we say then? Is the Law sin? May it never be! On the contrary, I would not have come to know sin except through the Law; for I would not have known about coveting if the Law had not said, "You shall not covet." (Romans 7:7 NASB)

The problem was on the human side of the covenant. The Law set the proper guidelines and was not too difficult to obey, but people simply did not want to obey it. It was not that they *could* not obey; it was that they *would* not. Sin became alive and took hold.

> But sin, taking opportunity through the commandment, produced in me coveting of every kind; for apart from the Law sin is dead. And I was once alive apart from the Law; but when the commandment came, sin became alive, and I died; and this commandment, which was to result in life, proved to result in death for me; for sin, taking opportunity through the commandment, deceived me, and through it killed me. (Romans 7:8-11 NASB)

In one sense, however, the Law did have a problem. Although it was holy and good, it could not change a person's will; it could not do anything about man's inner desire to do as he pleased, to act according to his self-interest. The writer of Hebrews agrees.

> For, on the one hand, there is a setting aside of

> a former commandment because of its weakness and uselessness (for the Law made nothing perfect), and on the other hand there is a bringing in of a better hope, through which we draw near to God. (Hebrews 7:18-19 NASB)

The Law made nothing perfect. It could not change a person on the inside. That's why it had to be set aside, not because it lacked goodness, but because it lacked power, the power to change a person's will. The book of Hebrews continues this theme.

> For the Law, since it has only a shadow of the good things to come and not the very form of things, can never by the same sacrifices year by year, which they offer continually, make perfect those who draw near. (Hebrews 10:1 NASB)

Since the Law could not perfect those who offered the Law's demanded sacrifices, it had to be replaced. Jesus, the great high priest, offered himself as the ultimate sacrifice to take the place of the animal sacrifices. He also replaced the priests who spilled blood and burned flesh on the altar and thereby gained no lasting internal effect for the people.

> Then he said, "Behold, I have come to do thy will." He takes away the first in order to establish the second. By this will we have been sanctified through the offering of the body of Jesus Christ once for all. And every priest stands daily ministering and offering time after time the same sacrifices, which can never take away sins; but he, having offered one sacrifice for sins

for all time, sat down at the right hand of God, waiting from that time onward until his enemies be made a footstool for his feet. For by one offering he has perfected for all time those who are sanctified. (Hebrews 10:9-14 NASB)

The writer of Hebrews has explained the cure, the antidote for Self Disease. The offering of Jesus Christ does what the Law could not do; it makes perfect those who follow him. It destroys the natural bent toward sinful self-will by means of a sacrifice in which his people participate. The Apostle Paul explains this miracle cure in his stunning treatise on how we can live in freedom from sin.

> What shall we say then? Are we to continue in sin that grace might increase? May it never be! How shall we who died to sin still live in it? Or do you not know that all of us who have been baptized into Christ Jesus have been baptized into his death? Therefore we have been buried with him through baptism into death, in order that as Christ was raised from the dead through the glory of the Father, so we too might walk in newness of life. For if we have become united with him in the likeness of his death, certainly we shall be also in the likeness of his resurrection, knowing this, that our old self was crucified with him, that our body of sin might be done away with, that we should no longer be slaves to sin; for he who has died is freed from sin. Now if we have died with Christ, we believe that we shall also live with

him, knowing that Christ, having been raised from the dead, is never to die again; death no longer is master over him. For the death that he died, he died to sin, once for all; but the life that he lives, he lives to God. Even so consider yourselves to be dead to sin, but alive to God in Christ Jesus. (Romans 6:1-11 NASB)

True Christians, those who have participated in the death of Christ, have died to sin and are thereby freed from its controlling power. This wonderful fact gave Paul reason to state his dramatic rhetorical question, "How shall we who died to sin still live in it?" In other words, we are not able to live in sin, because the old sinful self is dead and gone. The cure has been applied. What the Law could not do, God did, killing that indwelling principle of sin through the death of Christ, our ultimate high priest.

For the law of the Spirit of life in Christ Jesus has set you free from the law of sin and of death. For what the Law could not do, weak as it was through the flesh, God did: sending His own Son in the likeness of sinful flesh and as an offering for sin, He condemned sin in the flesh in order that the requirement of the Law might be fulfilled in us, who do not walk according to the flesh, but according to the Spirit. (Romans 8:2-4 NASB)

Without this cure for Self Disease, people who recognize the goodness of the Law will not succeed in obeying its precepts. Why? Deep down, they really don't want to. As much as they claim to want to obey the Law, when decision time comes, they sometimes choose to disobey because they prefer to satisfy their desires. "My will be done" continues to echo through the years and holds sway whenever a person chooses to say "No" to God.

There is no other option. There is no excuse. Moses said that full obedience to the Law isn't too difficult. Therefore, disobedience is a matter of the human will, and the will must change. There must be a redirection, the satisfaction of desires transforming from a passion for pleasing self to a passion for pleasing God.

How does this happen? Christians have described the process as a rebirth, being born again, and so it is. As Jesus said, "Truly, truly, I say to you, unless one is born again, he cannot see the kingdom of God" (John 3:3 NASB).

Many Christians have rightly understood that this process comes about because of God's response to the faith of the one being reborn. The rebirth is a procedure originated in God and performed by God. It is not something we can do to ourselves.

What brings about rebirth? The answer is often left out of the explanation. When a person recognizes his Self Disease and appeals to God for the cure, God performs the spiritual surgery that cuts away the cords that bind his will.

> And in Him you were also circumcised with a circumcision made without hands, in the removal of the body of the flesh by the circumcision of Christ; having been buried with Him in baptism, in which you were also raised up with Him through faith in the working of God,

who raised Him from the dead. (Colossians 2:11-12 NASB)

Here, as in the Romans passage, Paul describes the death to self, the participation in the sacrifice of Christ, but here in the book of Colossians he tells of a surgical cutting away of the flesh, a flesh-ectomy, if you will. This spiritual circumcision is the removal of the cause of Self Disease, and God wields his holy scalpel to make contrite supplicants into true Christians.

As Paul notes again, "Now those who belong to Christ Jesus have crucified the flesh with its passions and desires" (Galatians 5:24 NASB). With that self-will cut away, its passions and desires go with it. The death of the flesh marks the death of an old way of life.

Yes, rebirth has a morbid prerequisite—death. And this death of self is too often ignored, leading to false conversions and continued slavery to self. Bypassing God's surgical hand leaves a potential convert with the cause of his disease still intact and brings only superficial relief, a feeling of emotional stirring that lifts his spirits for a season.

In his reverie, he makes joyous commitments to God, promises of fidelity and service. Soon, however, he is thrown back into reality as he finds sin to be an unconquerable foe. And this is the sad end for all who short circuit God's salvation plan, for without the removal of the flesh, a diseased soul is still bound to a self-pleasing tendency.

Now we see why many professing Christians are still in spiritual bondage. While calling God "Master," they still feel the self-will that woos them to fulfill their own desires. They follow their fleshly passions, but after their indulgence is satisfied, they feel heavy guilt, having once again failed to fulfill their earnest promises. They are pulled back in line by the Law of God that they honor as being holy and good. This Law has done its proper work, serving as a guideline for behavior, but, as I noted before, it could not change their hearts.

The tragedy is that most Christians are told that this ongoing battle is normal, that guilt is brought about by the conviction of the Holy Spirit and is part of the normal sanctification process. This explanation temporarily relieves their guilty feelings and falsely confirms their salvation, and they survive the painful pull of the correcting law, ready to serve God again. Yet, even as the guilt subsides, a gnawing pain persists. Why are they trapped in this cycle of failure and disappointment?

Deep down they know that something is wrong. Shouldn't the Christian life be more than this seesaw battle with sin? What happened to the promise of Scripture? "But in all these things we overwhelmingly conquer through Him who loved us." (Romans 8:37 NASB) and "I can do all things through Him who strengthens me." (Philippians 4:13 NASB) and "We know that no one who is born of God sins; but He who was born of God keeps him and the evil one does not touch him." (1 John 5:18 NASB) Someone might ask, "Why doesn't my life display this wonderful power so poignantly described as the normal way of life for a believer in Christ?"

Yet, these nagging questions are left unanswered. People continue in the struggle, because they are told by other church members, co-strugglers who share the same questions, that frequently losing battles is normal. They are unable to find any contradicting guidance, because if others confess that something essential is missing from their own spiritual lives, they will lose the security they hold dear. This is a tragedy, indeed, for, as Jesus said, "A blind man cannot guide a blind man, can he? Will they not both fall into a pit?" (Luke 6:39 NASB)

Even when a struggling person manages to obey God, he is still a slave to his passions. Why? Although he obeys God in some circumstances, deep down he wants to follow "My Will be Done," obeying when he feels the powerful pull of God's precepts, and yielding to temptation when satisfying a selfish urge is the greater desire. He follows the influence that presses him with more force. He obeys because, and perhaps only because, he knows the sting of the proverbial whip. He disobeys, on the other hand, when the pleasure of a sinful act overwhelms his fear or love of God. In all practical reality, he obeys only self, since he follows the path of lower pain and higher pleasure.

Again, all the while, Christians are told that this kind of struggle is normal. The result is a group of professing Christians who are still enslaved, though the Bible says that true Christians are set free.

> But thanks be to God that though you were slaves of sin, you became obedient from the heart to that form of teaching to which you were committed, and having been freed from sin, you

became slaves of righteousness. (Romans 6:17-18 NASB)

But now having been freed from sin and enslaved to God, you derive your benefit, resulting in sanctification, and the outcome, eternal life. (Romans 6:22 NASB)

And, not only that, the Bible tells us that our obedience is what proves us to be true Christians.

And hereby we do know that we know him, if we keep his commandments. He that saith, I know him, and keepeth not his commandments, is a liar, and the truth is not in him. (1 John 2:3-4 KJV)

And ye know that he was manifested to take away our sins; and in him is no sin. Whosoever abideth in him sinneth not: whosoever sinneth hath not seen him, neither known him. Little children, let no man deceive you: he that doeth righteousness is righteous, even as he is righteous. He that committeth sin is of the devil; for the devil sinneth from the beginning. For this purpose the Son of God was manifested, that he might destroy the works of the devil. Whosoever is born of God doth not commit sin; for his seed remaineth in him: and he cannot sin, because he is born of God. In this the children of God are manifest, and the children of the devil: whosoever doeth not righteousness is not of God, neither he that loveth not his brother. (1 John 3:5-10 KJV)

These words are to echo in our ears, "Let no man deceive you." Don't ever let these words be snatched by the birds of the air who would steal the word of God before it can take root (Luke 8:5). These birds are not always easy to spot. They take many forms, even wearing the frocks of preachers, but they have one characteristic in common that is unmistakable. They deny the power of God with regard to godliness, as the Bible warns:

> But realize this, that in the last days difficult times will come. For men will be lovers of self, lovers of money, boastful, arrogant, revilers, disobedient to parents, ungrateful, unholy, unloving, irreconcilable, malicious gossips, without self-control, brutal, haters of good, treacherous, reckless, conceited, lovers of pleasure rather than lovers of God; holding to a form of godliness, although they have denied its power; and avoid such men as these. (2 Timothy 3:1-5 NASB)

Some do this unwittingly, teaching doctrines of Christian weakness merely because they were taught the same thing themselves. There is hope for them as the blinders are removed by the truth of God's word.

Unfortunately, some deny the power of godliness because of selfish motivations. Like the word-snatching birds, they are "lovers of pleasure rather than lovers of God." They live "My Will be Done" even though they profess to be Christians. They are lovers of self, and they have never undergone God's surgery, the removal of that self-serving influence called the flesh.

They love themselves more than the one who is supposed to be their master, and their behavior proves it.

In a way, the true believer also follows the maxim, "My Will be Done." He chooses to make his will the same as God's. The fulfilling of God's purpose is exactly what he wants to do. That's why there is no struggle to follow God's will. The flesh has been crucified and surgically removed. All reasons for doing anything opposing the will of God have been taken away by God. The Self Disease has been cured. The flesh has been replaced by the indwelling Holy Spirit who guides true believers into all truth.

As Paul wrote:

> "I have been crucified with Christ; and it is no longer I who live, but Christ lives in me; and the life which I now live in the flesh I live by faith in the Son of God, who loved me, and delivered Himself up for me." (Galatians 2:20 NASB)

Jesus is our perfect example. He also wanted only the will of his father. Even during his most trying temptation he said, "My Father, if it is possible, let this cup pass from me; yet not as I will, but as thou wilt." (Matthew 26:39 NASB) Although his physical body wilted at the prospect of suffering the horrible torture of crucifixion, Jesus fully conformed his own will to that of the Father. He was not saying that he had a desire to do something contrary to the will of his father; he was asking for God's will to be done, whether it be in God's will to let the cup pass from him or not.

In the same way, a Christian always chooses to

conform his will to the will of God, though he might, as Jesus did, experience trials along the path that God wants him to walk. For example, we might wonder if God really wants us to risk the dangers of the mission field. We might say, "God, if I don't have to live in that malaria-infested swamp, I would appreciate it if you would find some other way for me to reach those people. Nevertheless, if that's what you want, I am willing to go." When decision time comes, we want only what God wants. There is no struggle. God can trust us to obey. There is no need for a stinging whip to bring us in line. We are free indeed.

CHAPTER 3

After All, We're Only Human

What are we to conclude? Simply this—true Christians have been set free from sin and made alive to God. We don't have to sin any longer. In fact, any sin is a sign that we haven't really been set free by the power of the Holy Spirit, liberated from the selfish desires we cherished while being led by the flesh. Being Christians, we are supposed to live the rest of our lives in complete obedience to God.

When the realization of this lofty standard sinks in, some people might cry out, "What? Are you nuts? Don't you understand that I'm only human? I can't be like God."

"Being human" is the excuse of the generations, giving pardon to hundreds of foibles ranging from non-sinful habits, like biting fingernails, to depraved sinful behavior, like long-term adultery. The phrases continue to pour forth; "Nobody's perfect," "We all have our vices," "Everyone has their flaws," and on and on, until the pardon extends to every creature for every crime.

The excuses begin to sound like the rapid-fire defense of a child caught in an infantile misdeed. "But I didn't know I couldn't ride my skateboard in the kitchen." or "I forgot that you said I couldn't have ice cream for breakfast." The appeal to lack of knowledge or lack of ability is pervasive, possibly because it has been so effective in gaining a free pass for almost any forbidden activity.

Even adultery is excused by some as the unavoidable activity of us mere mortals. I am not exaggerating. During President Bill Clinton's impeachment uproar in Congress, Missouri Representative Richard Gephardt, speaking as the highest-ranking Democrat in the House of Representatives, said,

> Our founding fathers created a system of government of men, not of angels. No one standing in this House today can pass a puritanical test of purity that some are demanding. If we demand that mere mortals live up to this standard, we will see our seats of government lay empty, and we will see the best, most able people unfairly cast out of public service.
>
> We need to stop destroying imperfect people at the altar of an unattainable morality. We need to start living up to the standards which the public, in its wisdom, understands that imperfect people must strive for, though too often we fall short. We need to start healing. We need to end this downward spiral which will culminate in the death of representative democracy. [1]

Mr. Gephardt said, in effect, that no man can live without committing the immoral acts of an adulterer

---

[1] Source: An Even Better Place, by Dick Gephardt, p. 9-10 July 2, 1999

like President Clinton. Why? Because he is a "mere mortal." By this one excuse, all corrupt behavior becomes exonerated rather than excoriated, leading to the moral corruption of an entire nation. For if a leader of a people is allowed to sin without consequences, the entire population will suffer from the evil he normalizes. The depths to which a culture can fall, simply by excusing itself as being merely mortal, is chilling.

Although it is true that no human is perfect in physical attributes or in applied skills, for some reason "being human" has been equated to acting sinfully. Indeed, our physical urges and desires can bring about temptations to sin, but the characteristics of humanity itself do not force the act of sin. Aching hunger can lead to gluttony, exposure to the elements can lead to covetousness, and flaming sexual desire can lead to fornication, but these responses are not inevitable. No urge of human nature necessitates a sinful response.

On the flip side, the pangs of loneliness can arouse a call to God for fellowship, the dread of mortality can draw us closer to the hope of heaven, and the fear of the dark unknown can drive us to the light of God's word. Every aspect of our weakness can help us reach out for the strength that God provides rather than for indulgence in the flesh. While we recognize the explosive power of human emotions and their ability to wreak havoc, we also realize the awesome potential of a spirit-controlled passion.

The contagious hate personified in one Nazi propelled a killing machine throughout Europe, but in a different era the dogged determination of a Nile-born prophet sent a wave of Jewish humanity to freedom in the Promised Land. The perverted religious fervor of a power-hungry Arab scorched the bodies of innocent thousands as winged missiles buckled two concrete-and-steel towers, but the God-fearing preaching of one sea-soaked prophet brought Nineveh to its knees. The untamed debauchery of a mad emperor fed the flesh of valiant Christians to the lions of Rome, while the relentless love for the Gentiles by one tenacious apostle poured the good news of the Jewish Messiah into a spiritually starved world.

Yes, the power of human emotions can forever scar a culture, deeply wounding entire nations for centuries, but in the hands of God, those same emotions can be molded into mighty weapons of righteousness. The God who took the zeal of a murderous Pharisee and tamed his bloodthirsty passion to mold him into the Apostle of love is the same God who can take our humanity, our anger, our anguish, the deepest longings of our souls and transform them into holy passions. It is not our humanity that drags our souls toward hell or guides them toward heaven; it is how we brandish its fervor.

The Bible teaches that humans, with few exceptions, have sinned, giving rise to the belief that the inevitability of sin must have its cause in humanity itself. This cannot be true. Jesus was human, yet he did not sin. If the human condition demands sinful behavior as a necessary attribute, then either Jesus was not fully human or he must have sinned. There is no other possible conclusion.

But wasn't Jesus different? Wasn't he also divine, fully human and also fully God? Yes, this is true, but the divinity of Christ does not change the argument or the resulting conclusion. If fully human means sinful, then if Jesus was human, he was also sinful. The Bible teaches, however, that Jesus lived a sinless human life.

> Since then the children share in flesh and blood, he himself likewise also partook of the same, that through death he might render powerless him who had the power of death, that is, the devil; and might deliver those who through fear of death were subject to slavery all their lives. (Hebrews 2:14-15 NASB)

> For we do not have a high priest who cannot sympathize with our weaknesses, but one who has been tempted in all things as we are, yet without sin. (Hebrews 4:15 NASB)

It was the humanity of Christ that allowed him to fulfill the requirement of the Law. He proved that a human could live according to God's law, that is, a human who is guided by God's spirit rather than by his flesh.

In this quality lies the difference between the rest of mankind and Jesus Christ. All were fully human, but Christ had a nature that was bent only toward doing the will of God the Father, as he stated,

> Jesus said to them, "My food is to do the will of him who sent me, and to accomplish His work." (John 4:34 NASB)

> I can do nothing on my own initiative. As I hear, I judge; and my judgment is just, because I do

not seek my own will, but the will of Him who sent me. (John 5:30 NASB)

For I have come down from heaven, not to do My own will, but the will of Him who sent Me. (John 6:38 NASB)

Everyone else, as we saw in the previous chapter, was born with a bent toward self-gratification that became sinful when it veered away from the known law of God. The key to escaping this bent is to be transformed into the likeness of Christ through the power of his spirit, and this is exactly what happens when a convert joins in Christ's death. It is not our humanity that hinders us from perfectly obeying God; it is our lack of his abiding presence, the lack of his indwelling Holy Spirit who transforms our nature into one like Christ's.

> For those who are according to the flesh set their minds on the things of the flesh, but those who are according to the Spirit, the things of the Spirit. For the mind set on the flesh is death, but the mind set on the Spirit is life and peace, because the mind set on the flesh is hostile toward God; for it does not subject itself to the law of God, for it is not even able to do so; and those who are in the flesh cannot please God. However, you are not in the flesh but in the Spirit, if indeed the Spirit of God dwells in you. But if anyone does not have the Spirit of Christ, he does not belong to Him (Romans 8:5-9 NASB).

The teaching is clear. Christians have the Spirit of Christ, so we set our minds on the things of the Spirit. We had at one time set our minds on the things of the flesh, but no longer, and the difference is the indwelling presence of the Holy Spirit. We remain human, but we take on the likeness of Christ, being rid of the bent toward the flesh. And Paul sums up his conclusions as follows:

> So then, brethren, we are under obligation, not to the flesh, to live according to the flesh— for if you are living according to the flesh, you must die; but if by the Spirit you are putting to death the deeds of the body, you will live. For all who are being led by the Spirit of God, these are sons of God. (Romans 8:12-14 NASB)

If a person is living according to the flesh, that is, still sinning, he must die. If a person is being led by the Spirit, that is, not sinning, he is truly a son of God and has eternal life. As Paul says in Romans 6:23, "For the wages of sin is death, but the free gift of God is eternal life in Christ Jesus our Lord."

What does this mean for the person who bemoans his condition, thinking that being human makes him too weak to perform this high calling? It probably means that, still being led by the flesh, he has no concept of any other life. Being enslaved to his physical members, he cannot imagine being set free. A person who has known only prison cannot possibly imagine the benefits of living in a free society. Armed guards continually shadow his dreams, and iron bars forever mask his horizons.

The animal kingdom illustrates this phenomenon. Creatures who have been contained all of their lives, when finally set free, often limit their movement to the area of their former containment. Goldfish sometimes swim in circles after being released from a bowl, and birds that had a leg tied to a pole continue to march around it even after their bonds are broken. They have never known anything else.

There is good news for all who can see only through the mask of cruel slavery, who have never experienced the freedom of perfect obedience to God, who cannot imagine living outside of the toil of sin, the cruel taskmaster. The death and resurrection of Jesus Christ provides true freedom—freedom from sin and from slavery. As Jesus himself said,

> The Spirit of the Lord is upon me, because he anointed me to preach the gospel to the poor. He has sent me to proclaim release to the captives, and recovery of sight to the blind, to set free those who are downtrodden. (Luke 4:18 NASB)

Paul cried out from his bondage to sin: "Wretched man that I am! Who will set me free from the body of this death?" (Romans 7:24 NASB), and he supplied the answer three verses later, "For the law of the Spirit of life in Christ Jesus has set you free from the law of sin and of death" (Romans 8:2 NASB).

And Jesus summed up his yoke-breaking miracle, his reason for coming to earth, with this dramatic proclamation:

> Truly, truly, I say to you, everyone who commits sin is the slave of sin. And the slave does

not remain in the house forever; the son does remain forever. If therefore the Son shall make you free, you shall be free indeed. (John 8:34-36 NASB)

Here is the greatest news that we could possibly hear, that Jesus Christ, the Son of God, holds the keys to the prison doors. He has the power to set sinners free, and it is true freedom, as he said, "you shall be free indeed." But people must take note of his premise, "everyone who commits sin is the slave of sin." That phrase must mean that if Jesus sets someone free, then that person no longer sins. Committing sin is proof of enduring slavery.

This freedom is not a deathbed liberation that grants liberty as we exit our mortal frames, nor is it the result of painstaking years of monk-like sacrifice. Actual, practical freedom from sin is given to every surrendering soul, to every man who pulls the helmet of salvation over his head, to every woman who wears the lamb's holy white, to every child who hides his soul in the robes of his loving shepherd.

This is a promise from the mouth of Christ himself, "If therefore the Son shall make you free, you shall be free indeed."

John Wesley agreed:

A Christian is so far perfect as not to commit sin. This is the glorious privilege of every Christian, yes, though he be but a babe in Christ.[2]

---

[2] John Wesley, "A Plain Account of Christian Perfection", The Works of John Wesley, 11:376.

Perfect in relationships? No. Perfect in speaking? No. Perfect in obedience to God? A resounding Yes!

This fact is paramount. It brings stunning news to the majority of professing Christians who believe that sinning is a normal part of the Christian life. This fact might offend, it might frighten, it might bring anger, it might threaten security, yet it remains a fact. Being human is not an excuse for sin. The power to be born again, to live in the house of God's son is available to all. And being born of God means that God's holy seed abides in us, making the old sinful state null and void.

> Whosoever is born of God doth not commit sin; for his seed remaineth in him: and he cannot sin, because he is born of God. In this the children of God are manifest, and the children of the devil: whosoever doeth not righteousness is not of God, neither he that loveth not his brother. (1 John 3:9-10 KJV)

Many theologians have tried to weaken this passage, and who can say why? Are they still enslaved by their flesh so that they cannot possibly see how the straightforward meaning of this passage can be true? They often appeal to the present tense and translate the first verse in a way that connotes habitual, ongoing sin, such as "does not practice sin," somehow pretending that it means Christians don't continually sin.

First, no one continually sins; it is simply not possible. The text literally says, "No one who is born of God is doing a sin." Therefore, if anyone is doing a sin, then he is not born of God. This is an identifying characteristic of a Christian.

Second, if it means something other than doing any

sin at all, the sense of the entire passage is destroyed. In other words, if some degree of sinning is allowed in one born of God, then John has uttered nonsense. Why? It says by this the children of God and the children of the devil are made manifest, that is, we can tell who is and who is not a true believer by whether or not a person sins or does righteousness. How much sin can a person commit before he can be said to be an unbeliever? How low does the number of sins have to be for everyone to agree that a person committing them is a believer?

The truth is that any proposed number would be arbitrary and based on a person's experience and the experiences of the culture of the day. The only measure that is obvious for all times in any circumstances is whether or not a person sins at all.

Even if a person sins infrequently it proves that he is his own master, obeying Christ when it is convenient or disobeying when it is too difficult to follow the one who should be his master.

John Wesley agrees again:

> Indeed it is said, this means only, He sinneth not wilfully; or he doth not commit sin habitually; or, not as other men do; or, not as he did before. But by whom is this said? by St. John? No: There is no such word in the text; nor in the whole chapter; nor in all his Epistle; nor in any part of his writings whatsoever. [3]

A passage I quoted earlier has the same force:

---

3 John Wesley, "Christian Perfection", The Works of John Wesley, 6:6.

And by this we know that we have come to know Him, if we keep His commandments. The one who says, "I have come to know Him," and does not keep His commandments, is a liar, and the truth is not in him. (1 John 2:3-4 NASB)

The simple meaning is the correct meaning, and any effort to insert words such as *continually* or *habitually* effectively destroys the passage. If any sin is allowed, then there is no effectual force in, "And by this we know that we have come to know Him." Why? With no absolute guide as to how much sin is allowed, there is no way to know.

Even in our humanity, even with our longings, our hungers, and our deep-seated passions, we can always respond to God with love, dedication, and perseverance. Let no one deceive you. Do not let anyone tell you that just because you are prone to mistakes that you are also prone to sin.

The best typists miss a keystroke now and then, the greatest baseball players fail to get a hit most of the time, and no one can live without eventually aging and dying. There are true imperfections that correspond with our human condition. Obedience, however, is a choice, a conscious decision, one that can always and forever be accomplished without error. This is a gift from God, the promise of Christ, the seal of our salvation, the ever-present, powerful, sanctifying, indwelling Holy Spirit.

As Jesus said, "If you love Me, you will keep My commandments." (John 14:15 NASB)

No one can truthfully say that he loves God and still sin. Sinning proves a lack of love for God. It proves love for self and for the pleasures of sin. A common mantra from professing Christians goes something like this, "I still sin, but I hate my sin." This cannot be true for a Christian. Doing something you hate proves an enslaved state, and Christians are free from slavery to sin.

Here is a logical progression:

Premise #1: Christians love God, so they don't want to sin. (John 14:15 as stated above)

Premise #2: God provides Christians the power to resist and escape temptation.

> No temptation has overtaken you but such as is common to man; and God is faithful, who will not allow you to be tempted beyond what you are able, but with the temptation will provide the way of escape also, so that you will be able to endure it. (1 Corinthians 10:13 NASB)

Conclusion: Christians will successfully resist and escape temptation for two reasons: #1 - They love God and #2 - God provides them with the power to avoid sin.

There is no reasonable argument against this truth. If we love God and are also given the power to escape temptation to sin, then we will employ that power and avoid sin. The only reason to do otherwise would be because we don't really love God and love ourselves and sin instead.

The bottom line is that we can always obey God and avoid sin every day, every moment, for the rest of our lives.

Does your heart leap with joy at the prospect, or

do you despair at the hopelessness of what seems an unattainable goal? Some might even scoff, reciting rehearsed denials and rebuttals, refusing to see the simplicity of God's word, relying instead on their systems of doctrine for the sake of their security.

Whether you leap with joy or despair of hope, read on. The greatest of treasures awaits you. If you scoff, I urge you to consider the popular myths and how they have shipwrecked the church, and when you turn from them to God's unadulterated word, the light of truth might bring a new focus, a different angle, and maybe even a whole new way of life.

CHAPTER 4

A Righteous Reckoning

Jesus said to them, "My food is to do the will of Him who sent Me and to accomplish His work." (John 4:34 NASB)

A Parable

The ground seemed colder and harder than before. The morning dew dampened my dress, and the cold breeze gave me shivers. With Mama gone, Jimmy huddled close, half asleep in my arms, but the traffic on the bridge above us would soon awaken him. He could probably hear my stomach growling. It hurt, like someone drilling a hole right through it. But I couldn't cry, 'cause that would make Jimmy cry, too. If only Mama would come back with some thrown-away fruit. When was the last time I had an apple or a banana?

Ooooh! Thinking about food made the pain worse. I even imagined I could smell it, barbecued meat and buttered potatoes and warm bread.

No, it was too strong to be a dream. It was—

"Good morning!" A tall, well-dressed man stood in the shadow of our bridge. He carried a tray covered with meats, fruits, vegetables, and breads.

"Who are you?" I asked.

"I am the son of the owner of a fine restaurant at the corner across the Interstate." His long finger pointed toward a city block where I sometimes wished I could go to beg. "I brought all this delicious food, the fabulous dishes I prepare. I wanted you to see them so you could understand how wonderful the food is in our restaurant."

I clapped my hands. "Ohhh! It looks wonderful! Please, may I have some for Jimmy and me?"

"Have some? Here? Now? Oh, dear child, no. You are not in the restaurant. I just wanted you to see the food and smell it so you can know what it would be like to be with me at the restaurant. Let that thought keep you warm and filled." He picked up a plate from the tray. "This one is for you. It has roast beef, mashed potatoes and gravy, tender baby carrots, and a thick slice of hot buttered bread." He pointed at another plate on the tray. "That one is Jimmy's, a heaping pile of barbecued chicken, candied yams, corn on the cob, and a buttery biscuit."

My mouth watered. "We can't have any right now? Not even a bite?"

The man laughed softly. "Heavens no! It's all yours though, reserved for you at the restaurant. When the owner looks out over the highway, he sees you and smiles, knowing that you're warm and well fed, because all of this food is yours." He patted me on the head. "Doesn't it make you feel better to know that these scrumptious dinners are credited to you and that you have been declared fully fed?"

I ducked away from his hand. "*Should* it make me feel better?"

"Of course. It's reserved for you. Since the owner declared that you have been fed, it must be true." He blinked at me as if surprised at my question. "You should be grateful to the owner for his generosity. He doesn't have to do this, you know."

"No. I guess he doesn't."

"And you can look forward to the day when you can sit with him and enjoy all the benefits of being at his restaurant. He told me himself that someday he will come here to bring you across the highway and into his warm, food-filled home."

I couldn't talk any more. I just sighed and stared at his curious smile. He reached out and mussed Jimmy's hair before turning with the food tray and leaving us behind. He got into a van marked, "Heaven's Restaurant," and drove away, merging into the busy traffic and disappearing from sight.

Jimmy tugged on my sleeve. "Who was that, Sis? Why didn't he let us have any of that food?"

I pointed to the sign in the distance. "Some guy from a restaurant across the highway. He says we can come there and eat if we want to."

"Can we go? I'm awfully hungry."

I looked at my legs. Although they were covered by dirt and soot, their skinny calves and knobby knees were still obvious. "Even with you holding me up, Jimmy, we could never make it across that street. There's just no way. But he said the owner will come and take us there someday."

"When?" Jimmy pushed a fist into his stomach. "I'm hungry now."

"He didn't say, Jimmy." I shook my head. "He didn't say."

An unbelievable story? Yes, of course. No restaurant owner in his right mind would be so heartless and cruel. No one would ever show a starving person the food he needs to survive and then take it away, declaring that the person has been fed while promising ultimate fulfillment at an indefinite time in an unreachable place.

Of course this parable is unrealistic. Yet, a popular and pervasive system of theology explains God's work of justification as just such a promise—credit without substance, perception without reality—displaying righteousness as a gift, yet withholding it from a sinful generation truly starving for its transforming purity.

In this system, Christians are merely "reckoned" as being righteous. The character of Christ is "imputed" to them by a legal declaration. Just as the restaurant owner sees these children as being fully fed because the food has been credited to them, God sees a believer as being righteous because the perfect righteousness of Christ is credited to his account.

John Calvin explains:

> Justified by faith is he who, excluded from the righteousness of works, grasps the righteousness of Christ through faith, and clothed in it, appears in God's sight not as a sinner but as a righteous man. Therefore, we explain justification simply as the acceptance with which God receives us into his favor as righteous men. And

we say that it consists in the remission of sins and the imputation of Christ's righteousness.[4]

Part of this statement is true; God does credit us with righteousness, as the Scripture teaches:

> For what does the Scripture say? "And Abraham believed God, and it was reckoned to him as righteousness." Now to the one who works, his wage is not reckoned as a favor, but as what is due. But to the one who does not work, but believes in him who justifies the ungodly, his faith is reckoned as righteousness. (Romans 4:3-5 NASB)

> Therefore also it was reckoned to him as righteousness. Now not for his sake only was it written, that it was reckoned to him, but for our sake also, to whom it will be reckoned, as those who believe in him who raised Jesus our Lord from the dead, he who was delivered up because of our transgressions, and was raised because of our justification. (Romans 4:22-25 NASB)

Paul's purpose was to show the way to gain this reckoning, that righteousness comes through faith and not by works. Righteousness is given only to those who believe, those who have faith in this gracious God who raised Jesus from the dead.

Yes, the credit of righteousness is given, but theologians err when they portray this credit as existing

---

[4] (Calvin's Institutes, 3.11.2)

only in God's heavenly bank account and not acting effectively in reality. There is nothing in this passage, nor in any other, that says believers are given only credit and not actual righteousness. In fact, the same letter to the Romans says the opposite. Believers are made experientially righteous because there is a real change, a transaction within that makes them righteous in reality.

> Or do you not know that all of us who have been baptized into Christ Jesus have been baptized into His death? Therefore we have been buried with Him through baptism into death, in order that as Christ was raised from the dead through the glory of the Father, so we too might walk in newness of life. For if we have become united with Him in the likeness of His death, certainly we shall be also in the likeness of His resurrection, knowing this, that our old self was crucified with Him, that our body of sin might be done away with, that we should no longer be slaves to sin; for he who has died is freed from sin. (Romans 6:3-7 NASB)

And Paul states this truth even more boldly in Galatians:

> Now those who belong to Christ Jesus have crucified the flesh with its passions and desires. (Galatians 5:24 NASB)

There is a real transaction, a crucifixion of the old man. We were undeserving, unable to work our way to heaven, without hope of attaining to the righteous standard that would allow us entry. Yet, God placed our sinful selves into Christ's death, killing the flesh with all of its evil passions. And not only is the flesh dead; it is gone: "And in Him you were also circumcised with a circumcision made without hands, in the removal of the body of the flesh by the circumcision of Christ." (Colossians 2:11 NASB)

Still, many theologians insist that this crucifixion is somehow not real, that it is a "positional" truth that has no effect in experience.

> The declaration that I have crucified the flesh has with it no actualizing power in terms of experience even though it is an honest evaluation in harmony with the person I now most deeply am.[5]

> Sanctification by the blood of Christ is eternal. It is not an experience; it is positional; it has to do with the new place in God's eternal favor occupied by every believer – an unchanging and unchangeable position, to which defilement can never attach, in God's estimation.[6]

Where does the Scripture limit the crucifixion within us to existing only in God's estimation, only in that strange non-biblical place called "positional"? The answer is simple; it is found nowhere in the Bible.

---

[5] Birthright, David Needham page 266 1979, Multnomah)

[6] Holiness, The False and the True, H. A. Ironside, page 50, 1988 Loizeaux Brothers

Yet, these theologians insist on explaining God's great work as one that has no real effect on earth.

The Bible states the opposite, that this transformation is effective in experience. In fact, it must be. See how Paul begins his explanation of our joining in Christ's death:

> What shall we say then? Are we to continue in sin that grace might increase? May it never be! How shall we who died to sin still live in it? Or do you not know that all of us who have been baptized into Christ Jesus have been baptized into His death? (Romans 6:1-3 NASB)

Paul posed a question, "How shall we who died to sin still live in it?" This is a question about real life, about real sin versus real righteousness. Dying to sin must have an effect on whether or not we live in sin. Otherwise, there is no reason for the question.

Because of this real effect, Paul went into detail about what dying to sin is all about. He explained that we can no longer live in sin because we died to sin in Christ. If our death with Christ and our resurrection into his righteousness are merely positional truths that do not result in real righteousness and holy living, they would not explain Paul's "May it never be!" They would not answer "How shall we who died to sin still live in it?" because positional righteousness allows for continued living in sin. The passage would not make sense. Paul would be providing a reason for real holiness that has no practical effect.

It would be as though someone asked, "Are we to continue to starve?" and then giving the answer,

"Of course not. We have empty boxes that are labeled as food." But how can empty boxes feed a starving person? Obviously, they can't. Yet, many theologians would lead us to believe that we have received an empty case labeled "righteousness" that has no experiential value, but still somehow answers Paul's question. We are somehow considered holy because God slapped a "Holy" label on us even though we really aren't actually holy. Such an understanding of reckoned righteousness is an insult to the apostle and all the Scriptures.

The reason righteousness is reckoned to us is actually quite easy to understand. It's because it's true. God doesn't run a phony bank account. He doesn't give credit for something that isn't there. God places righteousness on us in reality. The sins of the past are wiped clean. The old man who committed those sins is dead, and a new man is alive, a new creature in Christ. God sees us as righteous because he has made us righteous indeed. And Paul tells the church that this transformation makes actual righteousness expected behavior.

> Do not lie to one another, since you laid aside the old self with its evil practices, and have put on the new self who is being renewed to a true knowledge according to the image of the One who created him. (Colossians 3:9-10 NASB)

If laying aside the old self is not experientially effective, then what good would it do to give it as a reason for not lying? The Bible is filled with this type of instruction, telling us that God's work in transforming us is the reason for our ability to live in righteousness.

> Therefore do not be partakers with them; for you were formerly darkness, but now you are light in the Lord; walk as children of light (for the fruit of the light consists in all goodness and righteousness and truth), trying to learn what is pleasing to the Lord. (Ephesians 5:7-10 NASB)

> And He Himself bore our sins in His body on the cross, that we might die to sin and live to righteousness; for by His wounds you were healed. For you were continually straying like sheep, but now you have returned to the Shepherd and Guardian of your souls. (1 Peter 2:24-25 NASB)

> and may be found in Him, not having a righteousness of my own derived from the Law, but that which is through faith in Christ, the righteousness which comes from God on the basis of faith, that I may know Him, and the power of His resurrection and the fellowship of His sufferings, being conformed to His death; in order that I may attain to the resurrection from the dead. (Philippians 3:8-11 NASB)

And Jesus told us that our true, experiential righteousness is essential for our entry into heaven. "For I say to you, that unless your righteousness surpasses that of the scribes and Pharisees, you shall not enter the kingdom of heaven. (Matthew 5:20 NASB)

Jesus was not talking about heavenly, "positional"

righteousness. His listeners would not have interpreted his statement in that way. The context proves that they would have understood his statement as practical and experiential. As Jesus said in the verse immediately preceding, "Whoever then annuls one of the least of these commandments, and so teaches others, shall be called least in the kingdom of heaven; but whoever keeps and teaches them, he shall be called great in the kingdom of heaven."

Jesus was speaking about their actual behavior, not about God's perception of their righteousness in a heavenly bank account. Entry into God's kingdom is based on a righteousness that obeys all of his commandments, annulling not even one of them, and the character that begets experiential righteousness is bestowed upon us through faith in him.

The Bible is clear. Practical, experiential righteousness is the sign that someone has been born again.

> If ye know that he is righteous, ye know that every one that doeth righteousness is born of him. (1 John 2:29 KJV)

> Little children, let no man deceive you: he that doeth righteousness is righteous, even as he is righteous. He that committeth sin is of the devil; for the devil sinneth from the beginning. For this purpose the Son of God was manifested, that he might destroy the works of the devil. Whosoever is born of God doth not commit sin; for his seed remaineth in him: and he cannot sin, because he is born of God. In this the children of God are manifest, and the children

of the devil: whosoever doeth not righteousness is not of God, neither he that loveth not his brother. (1 John 3:6-10 KJV)

If this righteousness is positional only, then John's statements would have no use. It is impossible to see righteousness that is merely reckoned, so "let no man deceive you" would be a warning that no one could heed. "In this the children of God are manifest" would be a lie, for righteousness that is merely imputed is invisible, manifest only to God and not to us who might be deceived by religious pretenders. And John's claim, "he that doeth righteousness is righteous even as he is righteous" would also be a lie, for these theologians would maintain that no one is really holy on this earth, since the imputation of Christ's righteousness has no such experiential effect.

How did this myth concerning positional righteousness begin? Why would someone invent such an unscriptural idea? Although the historical roots of the doctrine can be traced, we can only guess the motivations of someone who would invent and propagate it throughout Christendom. Surely they belong to the group about which Paul warned, men who are "holding to a form of godliness, although they have denied its power; avoid such men as these." (2 Timothy 3:5 NASB)

The idea of positional righteousness has spread, not because of any logical or Scriptural support, but because it provides a soothing balm to the guilt-ridden masses, people who feel that they cannot live up to the high calling of Scripture. It gives them security without sacrifice, promises without purity, and comfort without commitment.

The easy road has long been the one most heavily traveled, the wide path that leads to destruction, because the presence of many footprints leads the travelers to a false sense of security. Holding a majority opinion provides comfort, because these people can't believe that so many of their fellow believers could be wrong.

Why do people fear the truth? For what purpose do they hide its power? When inquiring sinners examine the gospel of Christ, what are they seeking? Is it the fear of hell that drives them to find a smooth road to salvation? Do the pangs of guilt call out for relief, asking for an easy pill to swallow—sweet smelling snake oil disguised as a rigorous doctrinal remedy?

Or instead are our motivations pure? Do we fall on our knees in true surrender, humiliated in sin, crying out for the righteousness that will satisfy our starving souls? When we come to God for spiritual healing, he will not fill our minds with empty promises while leaving our souls aching for true righteousness. He will not leave our cups dry when we, as beggars for grace, reach them out for the cool, living water that will quench our thirst. By grace through faith, he will give us righteousness, both credited in heaven and fully operational on earth, imputed and functional, real sanctification without which no one will see the Lord (Hebrews 12:14 NASB).

What, then, are we to think about the millions of professing Christians around the world who follow the doctrine of empty, imputed righteousness? Are they really unbelievers who have been duped or have gladly accepted a watered-down gospel and are still on the highway to hell? Or are they true Christians who would act according to their indwelling righteousness if they would only believe in the transforming power available to them?

Paul seems to allow for ignorance to the truth in Romans chapter six, giving his readers instruction on the practical ramifications of being dead to sin.

> For the death that he died, he died to sin, once for all; but the life that he lives, he lives to God. Even so consider yourselves to be dead to sin, but alive to God in Christ Jesus. Therefore do not let sin reign in your mortal body that you should obey its lusts, and do not go on presenting the members of your body to sin as instruments of unrighteousness; but present yourselves to God as those alive from the dead, and your members as instruments of righteousness to God. For sin shall not be master over you, for you are not under law, but under grace. (Romans 6:10-14 NASB)

Paul is not trying to determine whether or not the ignorant ones are true believers. His goal is practical as he urges his readers to follow the truth he is revealing. If they obey his commands, their outcome is eternal life. If they do not heed his warnings, they will receive eternal death.

> Therefore what benefit were you then deriving from the things of which you are now ashamed? For the outcome of those things is death. But

now having been freed from sin and enslaved to God, you derive your benefit, resulting in sanctification, and the outcome, eternal life. For the wages of sin is death, but the free gift of God is eternal life in Christ Jesus our Lord. (Romans 6:21-23 NASB)

For those who are truly hungering and thirsting for righteousness, here is the truth they are seeking, that God has prepared a way for them to be freed from sin and raised to new life with Christ, here and now, not just in heaven. They must consider themselves dead to sin and alive to God. This is their reckoning, an active belief that a positional truth is also true in reality. It has practical value, destroying the mastery of sin and making professing believers into slaves of righteousness.

"But thanks be to God that though you were slaves of sin, you became obedient from the heart to that form of teaching to which you were committed, and having been freed from sin, you became slaves of righteousness." (Romans 6:17-18 NASB)

"Blessed are those who hunger and thirst for righteousness, for they shall be satisfied." (Matthew 5:6 NASB)

Do you hunger and thirst for righteousness and yet find it elusive? Do you really want to obey? Ask yourself; what is keeping you from following Christ with all your heart? What is more powerful than his Holy Spirit? Is there really any obstacle that can overcome God's sanctifying power?

If you are a hungering and thirsting believer who meditates on the Romans passage, prayerfully considering the message, you can find the satisfaction that your soul has so long desired. You can cry out with Paul, "Wretched man that I am! Who will set me free from the body of this death?" (Romans 7:24 NASB) and God will give his answer, "I will, dear child. 'For the law of the Spirit of life in Christ Jesus has set you free from the law of sin and of death.'" (Romans 8:2 NASB)

Consider yourself dead to sin, and you can cry out "I don't have to sin any more. I am free at last. Those manacles of slavery are finally shattered. I was hungry, and now I am filled. Thanks be to God! I now bear holy righteousness, and I will be Christ's slave forevermore."

This is good news, indeed. God has filled our hungering souls, and we are satisfied.

A question remains, however, about the condition of those who have been informed of this truth, yet still turn away from it, holding instead to the impotent form of godliness to which they have been indoctrinated. They claim to be Christians, but they still choose to sin. Since there is no power that can overcome God's power, their sin must be willful disobedience. The Scripture gives them no security, no promise of heaven, only dire warnings.

> For if we go on sinning willfully after receiving the knowledge of the truth, there no longer remains a sacrifice for sins, but a certain terrifying expectation of judgment, and the fury of a fire which will consume the adversaries. Anyone who has set aside the Law of Moses

dies without mercy on the testimony of two or three witnesses. How much severer punishment do you think he will deserve who has trampled under foot the Son of God, and has regarded as unclean the blood of the covenant by which he was sanctified, and has insulted the Spirit of grace? For we know Him who said, "Vengeance is Mine, I will repay." And again, "The Lord will judge His people." It is a terrifying thing to fall into the hands of the living God. (Hebrews 10:26-31 NASB)

What are we to do with these fallen children, deceived by theologians in the halls of empty promises? Dear believer, if you still sin, do not take this passage lightly. Do not twist it so that it applies to someone else. What will be your end if your heart is hardened to its message? Will you become satisfied with a life of outward Christianity mixed with the deceitfulness of inward sin, accepting as true the heavily trodden path to destruction? Will you be abandoned there, thrown into the fiery pits of hell along with the doctors of doctrine whom you believed so readily?

Flee the temptation to hide from this warning, for this torture will last forever. Why? Because such a person has insulted the Spirit of grace, committed the ultimate blasphemy by stating to the world, "Christ lives in me, yet I am still a sinner."

Is sin worth that much? Are all of the doctrinal gymnastics, performed in order to keep your favorite sins, worth your eternal soul? Will you continue to trust in the righteousness stored in a heavenly bank account, which is really a bankrupt blindness that imperils your entry into heaven?

Or will you instead surrender your soul? Will you make that ultimate sacrifice and give all of your carnality over to Christ to be truly cleansed? If you really hunger and thirst for righteousness, I beseech you, brethren, by the mercies of God, to present your body a living and holy sacrifice (Romans 12:1 NASB). He will do what he promised and break the chains of slavery, making you dead to sin and alive to God, in reality, forever.

The Parable Completed

Fingers combed through my hair. I turned. Another man crouched within reach, a food tray resting on the ground nearby. "You look hungry, child. I have brought food for you and your brother."

I half closed an eye. "You mean, we can eat here and now? We don't have to go to a restaurant?"

"Here and now. By all means, take your fill. The restaurant's food is yours, for the owner has seen you and has told me to come and satisfy your hunger."

Tears rolled down my cheeks. Jimmy had already started on the bread and thin-sliced meats. I picked up an apple with one hand while stuffing warm rolls into my pockets with the other.

The man laughed in a pleasant way. "I will return with more food tomorrow and the next day and the next, until one day I will take you to the restaurant where you will live with the owner forever."

I couldn't take my eyes off him. His face was so full of love and compassion. As the pain in my belly subsided, love for this man swelled in my heart. "Do you have to go? Can't we go with you now?"

"You may not come with me now, but I will never forsake you. Wherever you go, I will find you. I will always meet your needs."

I looked at Jimmy. He smiled at me through jelly-covered cheeks. Such joy! After so much hunger, we were filled. Our aching stomachs, once wrenching with agony, felt the soothing return of life-giving sustenance.

When we turned back to the food, the man was gone, but he left behind blankets, warm clothes, and a silver pitcher. I read a small note attached to the pitcher's handle. "The water I give you will never run dry." With this precious gift in my hands, I knew he would someday return.

CHAPTER 5

Covered or Cleansed?
The Tragedy of a Blind God

He who planted the ear, does He not hear? He who formed the eye, does He not see? (Psalm 94:9 NASB)

Once upon a time there lived a vain Emperor whose only worry in life was to dress in elegant clothes. He changed clothes almost every hour and loved to show them off to his people.

Word of the Emperor's refined habits spread over his kingdom and beyond. Two scoundrels who had heard of the Emperor's vanity decided to take advantage of it. They introduced themselves at the gates of the palace with a scheme in mind.

"We are two very good tailors and after many years of research we have invented an extraordinary method to weave a cloth so light and fine that it looks invisible. As a matter of fact it is invisible to anyone who is too stupid and incompetent to appreciate its quality."

The chief of the guards heard the scoundrel's strange story and sent for the court chamberlain. The chamberlain notified the prime minister, who ran to the Emperor and disclosed the incredible news. The

Emperor's curiosity got the better of him and he decided to see the two scoundrels.

"Besides being invisible, your Highness, this cloth will be woven in colors and patterns created especially for you." The emperor gave the two men a bag of gold coins in exchange for their promise to begin working on the fabric immediately.

Thus begins the insightful tale of "The Emperor's New Clothes" by Hans Christian Anderson, a classic that exposes the blindness of hopelessly vain or arrogant leaders. The story is powerful because it topples the proud by using the simple honesty of a child to strip the emperor of his imagined dignity.

As readers, we might wonder or even scoff at the foolishness of the emperor and his vulnerability to the con game played by these tailors. We might also claim that we wouldn't be as pretentious as those commoners who refused to acknowledge their view of naked royalty while the Godiva-like procession passed by. But the subtle brilliance of Anderson's story is such that he allows us to see an obvious deception in order to prepare us to detect the subtler and craftier deceptions in our own time and society. He warns us to be on the alert. Sometimes the emperor's folly is easy to recognize. Sometimes it is not.

Many of us have witnessed obvious deception when unscrupulous church leaders engage in immoral or illegal behavior while preaching against the very sins they commit. Such hypocrisy is easy to identify.

Yet, there is also a stealthier deception that is more common among leaders and followers alike, a reverse application of Anderson's story that, when examined in the light of reason and Scripture, actually makes the people of Anderson's account seem wise and noble by comparison. In this tragic tale, rather than an emperor on display in his birthday suit, it is the common people who allow themselves to be duped and who then parade naked in front of their fully clothed emperor.

Unfortunately, this tale is not an exaggerated fable. It is reality.

In the previous chapter we saw that the idea of an imputed but ineffective righteousness is an illusion. A parallel doctrine states that the sacrifice of Christ has brought about a covering for sin, a mask of sorts, ensuring that God does not see our continuing sin. He sees only Jesus. This imputed covering by Christ is the emperor's new clothes, or in this case, the commoners' covering that hides them from the emperor.

Is this belief popular in mainstream Christianity? It seems so. Having heard this teaching from the lips of numerous pastors and lay people, I decided to search the Internet to get an idea of how pervasive this teaching is. It didn't take long to find a large collection of quotes, and I have included a couple to illustrate a common pattern of thought.

> We have "put on" Christ. When God looks at us he doesn't see us; he sees Christ. We "wear" him. We are hidden in him; we are covered by him. As the song says, "Dressed in his righteousness alone, faultless to stand before the throne."[7]

---

7 Max Lucado, https://maxlucado.com/the-gospel-of-second-chances/

Now that we are positionally unified with Christ, our relationship with God has been changed from one of condemnation to one of righteousness. Because Christ's work and merit is accrued to us by virtue of our being in Christ, God sees us as He sees Christ. He no longer sees us in Adam, or even in our own personal sin, but in Christ's righteousness and life. [8]

(In the footnotes, I cannot guarantee that the links I provided will lead to the source web pages when this book is published.)

In the cases above, not one Scripture reference was given to prove that God doesn't see ongoing sin in a Christian. The notion of a blinded God is trumpeted as though it were an obvious fact, one that need not be proven.

The idea of sins being covered in some sense does have biblical backing, as Paul stated in the book of Romans.

> Blessed are those whose lawless deeds have been forgiven, and whose sins have been covered. Blessed is the man whose sin the Lord will not take into account. (Romans 4:7-8 NASB)

This Romans passage is a quote from a psalm of David.

> How blessed is he whose transgression is forgiven, whose sin is covered! How blessed is

---

[8] The Believer's Union With Christ, Jason Dulle, https://www.onenesspentecostal.com/unionchrist.htm

the man to whom the LORD does not impute iniquity, and in whose spirit there is no deceit! (Psalm 32:1-2 NASB)

It is true that God "covers" sin, and our covering is provided by the sacrifice of Christ, but this does not mean that God somehow becomes blind to ongoing sin.

In both the Romans passage and in David's psalm the idea of covering is simply the choice not to take sin into account, to refrain from delivering deserved punishment. Far from implying that God doesn't see his sin, David goes on in his psalm to say,

> When I kept silent about my sin, my body wasted away through my groaning all day long. For day and night Thy hand was heavy upon me; my vitality was drained away as with the fever heat of summer. I acknowledged my sin to Thee, and my iniquity I did not hide; I said, "I will confess my transgressions to the Lord"; and Thou didst forgive the guilt of my sin. (Psalm 32:3-5 NASB)

If God didn't see David's sin, then his hand would not have been heavy upon David. Surely God did see it, and because of David's confession, God covered the sin. He did not take the sin into account. God forgave him.

This was the oft-repeated pattern of behavior under the old covenant: sin, feel conviction, confess, repent, and receive forgiveness. The same was true for David. If he committed another sin at a later time, that too would have brought about the heavy hand of God.

Without God's ability to see sin, conviction of sin in an old-covenant believer would likely never occur, nor would any resulting confession and repentance.

In these days under the new covenant, however, many church-goers have come to believe that, although they are now born-again Christians, they continue sinning, and God can no longer see their sinful actions. For some reason, God has become blind to reality, and when he casts his holy eyes our way he can see only Jesus. Even with absolutely no biblical foundation, this claim has become widely accepted. It has spread as a plague on Christianity.

God, our emperor, has become the blind fool in the eyes of his people. They believe he is not able to see his naked subjects as they parade around in their unashamed exposure. The tailors of this cheap gospel have convinced everyone that imputed righteousness is the finest of royal garb and that it covers their actions in the eyes of the all-seeing, all-knowing creator of the universe.

In Anderson's tale, the commoners could see that the king was naked. They just wouldn't admit it. In our story, does God see the clothes? His people are parading by him in sin. Can God tell what's going on? If he can, will he ignore it and pretend to be blind?

What does the Bible say about the claims of these gospel weavers? Does God really not see?

> Why do you say, O Jacob, and assert, O Israel, "My way is hidden from the LORD, and the justice due me escapes the notice of my God"? Do you not know? Have you not heard? The Everlasting God, the LORD, the Creator of the

ends of the earth does not become weary or tired. His understanding is inscrutable. (Isaiah 40:27-28 NASB)

But look, you are trusting in deceptive words that are worthless. Will you steal and murder, commit adultery and perjury, burn incense to Baal and follow other gods you have not known, and then come and stand before me in this house, which bears my name, and say, "We are safe"—safe to do all these detestable things? "Has this house, which is called by My name, become a den of robbers in your sight? Behold, I, even I, have seen it," declares the LORD. (Jeremiah 7:8-11 NASB)

Of course God sees. Of course the false tailors were lying. But how could such a stunning deception be pulled off on literally millions of professing Christians? Who are these con men who have so deftly swindled modern Christendom?

In many cases, they are well-respected teachers, and they speak these falsehoods in church circles. Pastors, counselors, and authors who desire to exonerate themselves have invented a way to ensure their own eternal security by weaving a lie that shoos away the heavy hand of God. "It's not God," they say, "it's Satan accusing me of sin. It can't be God. I'm covered. When God looks at me, he sees only Christ."

The Bible warned us that such teachers would come.

But false prophets also arose among the people, just as there will also be false teachers among you, who will secretly introduce destructive heresies, even denying the Master who bought them, bringing swift destruction upon themselves.

For speaking out arrogant words of vanity they entice by fleshly desires, by sensuality, those who barely escape from the ones who live in error, promising them freedom while they themselves are slaves of corruption; for by what a man is overcome, by this he is enslaved. (2 Peter 3:1, 18-19 NASB)

The visions of your prophets were false and worthless; they did not expose your sin to ward off your captivity. (Lamentations 2:14 NASB)

They dress the wound of my people as though it were not serious. "Peace, peace," they say, when there is no peace. (Jeremiah 8:11 NASB)

The church has been sold a bogus set of clothes by unscrupulous tailors—the teachers of a false gospel that promises freedom, yet ensnares its buyers in slavery. Witless buyers think that being told they are clothed in white robes is the same as actually wearing them. They believe God cannot see in them what they can so easily see in themselves and in each other. They believe that whether they wallow naked in the filth of immorality or commit less serious sins only on occasion, God looks down on them and smiles because he sees them in sparkling white robes, clothed in the image of his crucified son.

Such thinking is reprehensible. How can people so carelessly insult our holy, all-seeing, all-knowing Lord of the universe? God is not a foolish simpleton. He has no desire to play make-believe with his creation. He wants obedient people, not a self-deluded mirage.

Yet, some teachers have made God into a fool who looks down from heaven at a professing Christian in the act of adultery and says, "How nice. There's my beloved son, clothed in white. I'm sure he's obeying me." Lies and gossip fly into heaven, and all God hears is a sweet hymn of praise. The stench of hate and cruelty billow into the porticoes of paradise, and God thinks he's smelling the perfumed incense of a thanksgiving chorus.

Does that sound ridiculous? Of course it does. But this is the kind of teaching that has painted too many professors of faith in the scarlet colors of depravity, thereby crippling their ability to carry the light of Christ in this world.

If we allow this influence to spread, the visible church, the prophesied bride of Christ, will become soiled, refusing to clean herself up because of a perceived but false covering. Will Christ accept a dirty, naked harlot at the wedding altar, an adulteress who rejects the call to "Go and sin no more"?

No. A thousand times no. The Bible tells us that the true bride of Christ is far different.

> "Let us rejoice and be glad and give the glory to Him, for the marriage of the Lamb has come and His bride has made herself ready." And it was given to her to clothe herself in fine linen, bright and clean; for the fine linen is the righteous acts of the saints. (Revelation 19:7-8 NASB)

The bride of the Lamb is clothed in fine linen. And what is this clothing? It is the righteous acts of the saints, real obedience to God, not a blind perception of an imputed holiness that isn't manifested in day-to-day life.

How far have some people fallen to believe that all of these descriptions of cleanness, holiness, and righteousness are somehow not true, not real in practice? How could people be so gullible to believe these false teachers, the modern day tailors of invisible robes?

The situation is dire, but there is a solution. There is a way to become clean—washed and dressed in white linen—wearing robes that will make believers ready for the altar, ready to approach Jesus Christ as his holy bride.

> Because you say, "I am rich, and have become wealthy, and have need of nothing," and you do not know that you are wretched and miserable and poor and blind and naked, I advise you to buy from Me gold refined by fire, that you may become rich, and white garments, that you may clothe yourself, and that the shame of your nakedness may not be revealed; and eye salve to anoint your eyes, that you may see. (Revelation 3:17-18 NASB)

> 'But you have a few people in Sardis who have not soiled their garments; and they will walk with Me in white; for they are worthy. He who overcomes shall thus be clothed in white garments; and I will not erase his name from the book of life, and I will confess his name before

My Father, and before His angels. (Revelation 3:4-5 NASB)

But you did not learn Christ in this way, if indeed you have heard Him and have been taught in Him, just as truth is in Jesus, that, in reference to your former manner of life, you lay aside the old self, which is being corrupted in accordance with the lusts of deceit, and that you be renewed in the spirit of your mind, and put on the new self, which in the likeness of God has been created in righteousness and holiness of the truth. (Ephesians 4:20-24 NASB)

True Christians are not merely covered; they are cleansed, transformed into the likeness of Christ himself. God *sees* us as holy, because we *are* holy. When God looks at us, he sees Christ because Christ lives in us, and we act according to his nature. The clothing is true righteousness, the likeness of God in us.

What shall we say then to our church brethren who are caught wearing only make-believe clothes, people who rely on a sin covering that doesn't really exist? Let this resonate as an entreaty rather than a preachy sermon, as Paul beseeched the Corinthian church,

> "Therefore, we are ambassadors for Christ, as though God were entreating through us; we beg you on behalf of Christ, be reconciled to God. He made Him who knew no sin to be sin on our behalf, that we might become the righteousness of God in Him." (2 Corinthians 5:20-21 NASB)

If you are in sin, confess it to God and surrender

your soul to the one who died to make you holy. He will cleanse you from sin, as John teaches, "If we confess our sins, He is faithful and righteous to forgive us our sins and to cleanse us from all unrighteousness." (1 John 1:9 NASB) He cleanses us from all unrighteousness and sets us free.

Do not be fooled by teachers who would keep you in slavery to sin. True freedom in Christ is actually a threat to unscrupulous church leaders. Real followers of Christ are free, the veil is lifted, and they can see through the lies and deceit of the false prophets. They cannot be enslaved by the tailors of a false gospel, because they are bound to serve Christ alone. Their allegiance cannot be purchased at any price, because they belong to God.

A person who is truly free is not afraid to speak the truth, that sin is sin and that a naked man is naked.

Everyone said, loud enough for the others to hear: "Look at the Emperor's new clothes. They're beautiful!"

"What a marvelous train!"

"And the colors! The colors of that beautiful fabric! I have never seen anything like it in my life!" They all tried to conceal their disappointment at not being able to see the clothes, and since nobody was willing to admit his own stupidity and incompetence, they all behaved as the two scoundrels had predicted.

A child, however, who had no important job and could only see things as his eyes showed them to him, went up to the carriage.

"The Emperor is naked," he said.

"Fool!" his father reprimanded, running after him. "Don't talk nonsense!" He grabbed his child and took him away. But the boy's remark, which had been heard by the bystanders, was repeated over and over again until everyone cried:

"The boy is right! The Emperor is naked! It's true!"

The Emperor realized that the people were right but could not admit to that. He thought it better to continue the procession under the illusion that anyone who couldn't see his clothes was either stupid or incompetent. And he stood stiffly on his carriage, while behind him a page held his imaginary mantle.

Shall we follow in the footsteps of the foolish emperor? If we ourselves are found naked, shall we reject the truth? May it never be! Let us reach out and accept the holy robes that Christ so willingly offers. Surrender your soul to God, and he will dress you in true righteousness. Then, you will be free from sin, free indeed.

CHAPTER 6

What is the Gospel?

But now having been freed from sin and enslaved to God, you derive your benefit, resulting in sanctification, and the outcome, eternal life. (Romans 6:22 NASB)

In the previous chapters, I have taken an ardent stand against what I have called a false gospel, and I have contended for a true gospel that results in complete holiness in those who receive and submit to it. Yet, to this point I have not described exactly what that true gospel is.

Although the true gospel is clearly presented in the Bible, many teachers have perverted it to the point that even honest seekers of truth, in order to find the life-giving fruit, have to unravel knotted falsehoods that these teachers have foisted upon their followers.

For example, I am confident that many teachers have quoted the above verse without carefully noting the progression within its structure. First comes freedom from sin and servitude to God. From this freedom, people derive a benefit ("fruit" in the Greek). That benefit begins with sanctification. The outcome of sanctification is eternal life.

The order of events is thereby provided:

1. Freedom from sin and servitude to God.
2. Sanctification.
3. Eternal life.

The verse makes this order clear. For something to be derived, the thing from which it is derived must exist first. That thing is a prerequisite. Therefore, being freed from sin and enslaved to God comes before the benefit can be derived. As I mentioned before, the Greek word for "benefit" is fruit. You cannot have fruit without first having a source for the fruit, and that source is freedom from sin.

The same is true regarding an outcome. If eternal life is the outcome of sanctification, then sanctification is a prerequisite for eternal life. Sanctification must exist before the granting of eternal life.

Most Christian theologians believe that God grants eternal life first, and then a slow sanctification process occurs afterward. This is true in some sense, depending on the definition of sanctification. If sanctification is defined as growing in wisdom, knowledge, and experience, then sanctification does take place during our years as faithful followers of Christ.

In this context, however, sanctification is not progressive growth. It is the benefit derived from being freed from sin and enslaved to God. Sanctification involves behavior associated with someone who has been released from the chains of sin. Therefore, sanctification means to be obedient to God. It means ceasing from sin.

The outcome of this kind of sanctification is eternal life.

This is the bedrock foundation of the true gospel. Sin-free sanctification is required in order to gain eternal life. In other words, sanctification precedes justification, and justification is the scriptural equivalent of gaining eternal life.

Many professing Christians will balk at such a statement. Some will call it heresy. Yet, Paul states the matter plainly. The outcome of freedom from sin and sanctification is eternal life. Freedom from sin comes first. This is the heart of the gospel and the means by which we are saved, the pathway to the peace and joy of being forever with God in heaven.

For God to be just, he must punish a sinner for the sins he commits, as the verse that follows says, "For the wages of sin is death, but the free gift of God is eternal life in Christ Jesus our Lord."

A sinner must die for justice to be served. Therefore, in order to be forgiven, a person must no longer be a sinner.

Many teach that Jesus died to take the penalty for sin that we deserved. "He paid the debt," some sing in their choruses. Yet, the Bible makes no such statement. In fact, it is clear that Jesus did not pay the penalty that sinners deserve. The penalty is eternity in hell, and Jesus is not suffering in hell. He ascended to the right hand of the Father. Therefore, Jesus did not suffer the deserved penalty.

Also, Jesus did not pay our debt. Again, nothing in the Bible says that Jesus paid the debt for our sin. In fact, the Bible says that God canceled our debt.

> When you were dead in your transgressions and the uncircumcision of your flesh, He made you alive together with Him, having forgiven us all our transgressions, having canceled out the certificate of debt consisting of decrees against us, which was hostile to us; and He has taken it out of the way, having nailed it to the cross. (Colossians 2:13-14 NASB)

Since the debt was canceled, it was not paid. If someone paid the debt, then it was not canceled. This is a simple maxim. A paid debt is not canceled, and a canceled debt is not paid.

Why did God cancel the debt for a Christian? Because the sinner he once was has died. The person who sinned passed away. Paul stated this fact during his explanation leading up to the foundational statement of the gospel.

> For if we have become united with Him in the likeness of His death, certainly we shall also be in the likeness of His resurrection, knowing this, that our old self was crucified with Him, in order that our body of sin might be done away with, so that we would no longer be slaves to sin; for he who has died is freed from sin. (Romans 6:5-7 NASB)

It is unfortunate how the NASB and the KJV translate the last verse in this passage. The Greek says, "for he who has died is *justified* from sin." The ASV gets it right. It is the same Greek word translated as *justified* in many other places, such as: "Much more then, having now been justified by His blood, we shall be saved from the wrath of God through Him." (Romans 5:9 NASB)

The distinction is crucial in verse seven. Those who have died are justified—saved, forgiven of sin. Death is the reason God grants this justification and forgiveness.

Jesus did not die to suffer the penalty for our sin. He did not die to pay a debt. He died so that we could die with Him and be raised to new life.

Such a realization has enormous implications on a proper view of the atonement. Death is the reason we are justified. The person who sinned has died, and a new person has been born. It would be unjust for God to punish a person who is not the same person who sinned. And now he can justify this new person, because, in a very real way, that person has not sinned. There is no reason to punish him.

Therefore, the progression of salvation proceeds as follows:

1. Death with Jesus (the old self is killed)
2. Resurrection to new life with Jesus (a new creature is born)
3. Freedom from sin, servitude to God, and sanctification.
4. Justification (forgiveness) and eternal life

This explanation of the true gospel's atonement is also provided in Hebrews chapter ten. It begins with the statement of the inadequacy of the Law:

> "For the Law, since it has only a shadow of the good things to come and not the very form of things, can never, by the same sacrifices which

they offer continually year by year, make perfect those who draw near." (Hebrews 10:1 NASB)

The Law's sacrifices were unable to make people perfect. The next verse provides what the text means by "perfect."

Otherwise, would they not have ceased to be offered, because the worshipers, having once been cleansed, would no longer have had consciousness of sins? (Hebrews 10:2 NASB)

If the sacrifices had made people perfect, they would no longer need to offer sacrifices. They would no longer have consciousness of sins because they would have stopped sinning.

Therefore, the inadequacy of the Law is explained—it was unable to make people perfect in obedience. It could not make them sinless. Why? Verse four says, "For it is impossible for the blood of bulls and goats to take away sins." In other words, it is not possible for anyone to be changed spiritually or morally through the death of an animal.

Hereby the problem is stated. The Law couldn't make people perfect (sinless), because the sacrifices were inadequate to do so. Then the writer of Hebrews provides the solution:

Therefore, when He comes into the world, He says, "Sacrifice and offerings you have not desired, but a body you have prepared for me; in whole burnt offerings and sacrifices for sin you have taken no pleasure. Then I said,

'Behold, I have come (in the scroll of the book it is written of me) to do your will, O God.'"

After saying above, "Sacrifices and offerings and whole burnt offerings and sacrifices for sin you have not desired, nor have you taken pleasure in them" (which are offered according to the Law), then He said, "Behold, I have come to do your will." He takes away the first in order to establish the second. (Hebrews 10:5-9 NASB)

The new covenant was established by the obedience of the one who came to do God's will. And what does this will accomplish? Verse ten answers: "By this will we have been sanctified through the offering of the body of Jesus Christ once for all."

God's will brings about sanctification for all believers. We are set apart for Him.

How does that happen? The next three verses answer:

Every priest stands daily ministering and offering time after time the same sacrifices, which can never take away sins; but He, having offered one sacrifice for sins for all time, sat down at the right hand of God waiting from that time onward until His enemies be made a footstool for His feet. (Hebrews 10:11-13 NASB)

Instead of multiple offerings that cannot take away sins, Jesus provided a single offering for all time. And what did that one sacrifice do? Verse fourteen answers: "For by one offering He has perfected for all time those who are sanctified." (Hebrews 10:14 NASB)

This takes us back to the first verse. The Law could not make people perfect (sinless), but the offering of Jesus does. Remember, verse ten established that all believers are sanctified, so verse fourteen indicates that all believers have been perfected in righteousness. They have all ceased from sin.

The writer of Hebrews defines this as the new covenant:

> And the Holy Spirit also testifies to us; for after saying, "This is the covenant that I will make with them after those days, says the Lord: I will put my laws upon their heart, and on their mind I will write them," He then says, "And their sins and their lawless deeds I will remember no more." Now where there is forgiveness of these things, there is no longer any offering for sin. (Hebrews 10:15-18 NASB)

Now that we are forgiven, there is no longer an offering. Since we stopped sinning, there is no need of one.

Many theologians claim that Jesus' sacrifice provides forgiveness of sins that a person commits after salvation, but there is no hint of that concept here. In fact, the text contradicts such an idea. There was one sacrifice for the sins we committed in the past, and that sacrifice brought perfection. It took away sins. True believers do not commit sins after the sanctifying work that perfects them and places them under the new covenant.

This new covenant, sealed by the blood of a

one-time, perfect sacrifice, cleanses completely, perfects forever, and provides forgiveness.

How does someone enter this new covenant? How does a sinner die to self and become perfected by the one sacrifice, Jesus Christ? By taking on an obedient heart and being committed to our faith's teaching, as Paul explains in Romans six:

> "But thanks be to God that though you were slaves of sin, you became obedient from the heart to that form of teaching to which you were committed, and having been freed from sin, you became slaves of righteousness." (Romans 6:17-18 NASB)

The explanation continues:

> "For just as you presented your members as slaves to impurity and to lawlessness, resulting in further lawlessness, so now present your members as slaves to righteousness, resulting in sanctification." (Romans 6:19 NASB)

Presenting yourself to God as slaves to righteousness results in the sanctification that leads to justification and eternal life. In other words, you have to repent of and forsake sin, then turn to God with an obedient heart that commits all things to Him. This turning from a sinful way of life is, in essence, crucifying your old, sinful self. You spiritually share in the death of Christ, and God raises you from that death as a new creation, born again, cleansed from all unrighteousness.

There can be no holding back of any sin, any evil heart attitude, any shadow of unrighteous behavior.

Sin is a choice. Obedience is a choice. A sinner must choose by faith to no longer be a sinner.

Some will cry that this is salvation by works, but their cry is a false one. Sinners are slaves of sin, so when they repent and turn to God, they do so by faith, realizing that only God can unlock their chains. This surrender is a turning of the heart that reaches out to the one who can set sinners free from sin. They do no works to earn salvation, but they must turn their hearts from sin to obedience and ask God to perform the sanctifying work of killing the old self and raising a new creature to life.

This is the true gospel, and it honors God by telling the truth about his power to set sinners free, by telling the world that he loves people enough to break the chains of those who reach out to him by faith.

Let us reject the counterfeit gospel that cripples God's power, denies that he can cleanse from all sin, and reduces the new covenant to nothing more than a different label on old-covenant futility—a never-ending cycle of sin and repentance that produces unfaithful followers who rely on an impotent savior, a false Jesus who cannot save from sin.

The true gospel is far better than this weak excuse for atonement. The blood of Jesus does perfect His followers, thereby enabling them to be faithful forever. Let us march under this banner—a proclamation that honors God by telling of His power to make His people righteous in reality, that they are free indeed.

CHAPTER 7

It's All About Love

Upon hearing this explanation of God's provision for holiness, some people might become overly focused on not sinning. An obsession with this not-sinning idea can become a new law in their lives that might result in another form of bondage. In other words, "Don't sin" becomes a driving force instead of "Love God," and that can be a negative, debilitating false religion.

Jesus said, "If you love me, you will keep my commandments." Loving him is paramount. It is the priority. It is the fuel for the passion that results in a heart that obeys God. There is no need to focus on "Don't sin."

Yet, even if this is understood, some people might wonder about their actions. When they do something that they later learn was wrong and they come to regret it, was the past action a sin? By doing this questionable act, did they prove that they don't really love God or that they aren't true Christians after all? Or even worse, did they forfeit their salvation and are they now spiritually lost?

They are asking the wrong questions. They should instead be asking, "What was my thinking and motivation at the time of the action in question? Did I intend to violate a known law or principle of God? Or am I instead unfairly projecting my current understanding back on myself at a time that I didn't have the insight I have now?"

By such backwards-in-time projection, some people transform an honest mistake into a sin and then unfairly question themselves to the point of distraction or even despair.

A mistake is not a sin, and a sin is not a mistake. If we act in a way that we learn later was wrong, the past act was merely a mistake. If we act in a way that we know is wrong at the time of the act, that is a sin.

Sin is an act that violates the known will of God at the time of the act. As the Bible says, "Therefore, to one who knows the right thing to do and does not do it, to him it is sin." (James 4:17 NASB)

Notice that James says, "to him it is sin," not simply, "it is sin." Why? Because the action is not sin to someone who did not know the right thing to do. Therefore, knowledge of right and wrong is necessary for sin to occur.

As I stated earlier, if you gain knowledge that an action in the past was wrong, and you didn't have that understanding at the time, then the action was not a sin. Now armed with this knowledge, you will not commit this action again. Otherwise, it would then be a sin.

Embracing this concept is liberating. Past acts of ignorance will never cripple you. You will not allow them to cast doubt on your standing with God. You will know that you have not sinned. You have simply done something that you didn't know was wrong.

Some people point to passages like Leviticus 4:2

and Numbers 15:27-28 to try to prove that a person can sin unintentionally, but they err in defining what is truly unintentional. Refuting their points here, however, would cause this book to bog down far too much. It is sufficient to say that the New Testament clarifies the Old Testament and that sin is clearly defined for us who live under the new covenant. There is no unintentional sin in people who have the Holy Spirit of God dwelling within them. They will never be without a helper who guides them into all truth.

The bottom line is simple. We are spiritually free. As Paul stated, "It was for freedom that Christ set us free; therefore keep standing firm and do not be subject again to a yoke of slavery." Worrying about what is or is not sin can be an enslaving obsession.

We live under the law of love. As Jesus said, "You shall love the Lord your God with all your heart, and with all your soul, and with all your mind. This is the great and foremost commandment. The second is like it. You shall love your neighbor as yourself. On these two commandments depend the whole Law and the Prophets." (Matthew 22:37-40 NASB)

We love God. Therefore, we obey him. Love generates the passion to do exactly according to his will. If we know his will and choose to forsake it, then we prove that we don't really love God.

It's that simple.

We are not in slavery. We are sons of God. Since we love God, we do our Father's will, and we are not in bondage to a written law or a theological system. We are free indeed.

APPENDIX

Common Objections

Objection #1 – 1 John 1:8

Most professing Christians deny the necessity or even the possibility of living a sinless life after salvation. They often defend these denials by appealing to Scripture. The most common appeal is to 1 John 1:8. Theologians often quote this single verse and believe there is nothing more to be said. They believe it nullifies dozens of passages that teach the practical reality of sinless Christianity.

The problem is that they always quote the verse out of context, and they twist the verse to force a meaning that opposes what the passage actually teaches.

Here is the verse out of context:

If we say that we have no sin, we are deceiving ourselves and the truth is not in us." (1 John 1:8 NASB) And sometimes verse ten is also used. "If we say that we have not sinned, we make Him a liar and His word is not in us. (1 John 1:10 NASB)

Here is the context:

What was from the beginning, what we have

heard, what we have seen with our eyes, what we have looked at and touched with our hands, concerning the Word of Life-- and the life was manifested, and we have seen and testify and proclaim to you the eternal life, which was with the Father and was manifested to us-- what we have seen and heard we proclaim to you also, so that you too may have fellowship with us; and indeed our fellowship is with the Father, and with His Son Jesus Christ. These things we write, so that our joy may be made complete.

This is the message we have heard from Him and announce to you, that God is Light, and in Him there is no darkness at all. If we say that we have fellowship with Him and yet walk in the darkness, we lie and do not practice the truth; but if we walk in the Light as He Himself is in the Light, we have fellowship with one another, and the blood of Jesus His Son cleanses us from all sin. If we say that we have no sin, we are deceiving ourselves and the truth is not in us. If we confess our sins, He is faithful and righteous to forgive us our sins and to cleanse us from all unrighteousness. If we say that we have not sinned, we make Him a liar and His word is not in us. (1 John 1:1-10 NASB)

The first four verses state the reason for John's letter, to proclaim what he has witnessed so that his readers can have the fellowship of eternal life. He wants to proclaim the gospel message. Then, verses five through ten contain that message: "This is the message we have heard from Him and announce to you ..." and the gospel message follows to the end of the chapter.

Therefore, verses five through ten contain a message that conveys what is necessary to gain fellowship and eternal life.

John's first point is that God is light and there is no darkness in Him. That is the foundation of the gospel message.

The second point follows logically. If we say that we have fellowship with God and walk in darkness, obviously we are lying. Why? Because there is no darkness in God. This helps us see that "we" in this context cannot mean "only Christians," as some assert. Since fellowship with God is equated with having eternal life, the person who walks in darkness must not be a true Christian, so "we" cannot be "we Christians." The intent must be a larger "we," such as "we people," which works for every verse in this passage.

The third point also follows and adds a cleansing act. If we walk in the Light, we have fellowship with God and the blood of Christ cleanses us from all sin.

Remember, this is a gospel message designed to bring eternal life. John has established that if a person walks in the light, he will be cleansed of his sin and granted eternal life. Therefore, this passage is designed to show an unbeliever the way of salvation. An unbeliever must admit that he has sin in order to be cleansed. If he says he has no sin (verse eight), he is deceiving himself, and the truth is not in him.

This isn't about a Christian claiming to have no sin. It's about someone making this claim who still needs to be cleansed. If that's not the case, then verse seven would make no sense. It says that the blood cleanses from all sin. Sin is gone. What sin would be remaining? None. Did Jesus do an incomplete job in cleansing from all sin? Of course not.

Therefore, 1 John 1:8 doesn't say that Christians cannot claim sinlessness. The passage teaches the opposite. All Christians are cleansed from all sin. It is the one who hasn't been cleansed yet who cannot make a claim of sinlessness.

And verse nine provides the solution for the one who hasn't been cleansed yet: "If we confess our sins, He is faithful and righteous to forgive us our sins and to cleanse us from all unrighteousness." Again, this is a complete cleansing. Sin is removed. Verse nine is part of a gospel message that teaches what someone needs to do to be saved and gain the eternal life that John desires for his readers.

Read verses seven and nine. Does Jesus cleanse from all sin or not? Of course He does. Therefore, a Christian has no sin. Those who have not yet been cleansed need to confess their sins so that they, too, can be cleansed from all sin and be saved.

In short, this passage is a gospel message, and those who need initial cleansing are the ones in mind in verses eight and ten. The passage teaches complete sinlessness in those who are cleansed, and theologians who use this verse to prove that sinlessness is impossible in a Christian teach an interpretation that is the opposite of what the writer intended.

Also, simple logic proves my point. If verses eight and ten mean that it is improper to say you have completely stopped sinning, the "have no sin" and "have not sinned" phrases must have a definite time frame in mind. For example, if I say that I have not sinned in the past year, someone might say, "But 1 John 1:10 would call you a liar for saying that you have not sinned."

If, however, I changed the time frame and say that I have not sinned in the last ten seconds, would 1 John 1:10 apply? I am making the same kind of statement but with a different time claim. Many would say that it is reasonable to claim a sinless ten seconds. If even this is denied, the argument could be divided into microseconds, and the denier would have to admit that he could not claim a sinless fraction of time of tiny proportions.

In order to maintain this objection, a person would have to say that he is constantly sinning in every iota of time. This would mean that Christians are always sinning, in direct contradiction to numerous descriptions in Scripture of a Christian's actual behavior:

> We know that no one who is born of God sins; but He who was born of God keeps him, and the evil one does not touch him." (1 John 5:18 NASB)

> By this, love is perfected with us, so that we may have confidence in the day of judgment; because as He is, so also are we in this world. (1 John 4:17 NASB)

> By this we know that we have come to know Him, if we keep His commandments. The one who says, "I have come to know Him," and does not keep His commandments, is a liar, and the truth is not in him (1 John 2:3-4 NASB)

> What shall we say then? Are we to continue in sin so that grace may increase? May it never be! How shall we who died to sin still live in it? (Romans 6:1-2 NASB)

These false teachers would have to admit that they are never obedient. That's where the logic of their interpretation must take them.

The most reasonable interpretation of these verses is that if a person claims that he has never sinned, and because of this claim thinks that he does not need a cleansing savior, he is deceiving himself and makes God a liar, because he contradicts the scriptural teaching that everyone needs to be cleansed from sin by the atoning work of Christ.

Objection #2 – 1 John 2:1

Another passage commonly used to defend the concept of sinful behavior in Christians is the first verse of 1 John chapter two.

> My little children, I am writing these things to you so that you may not sin. And if anyone sins, we have an Advocate with the Father, Jesus Christ the righteous. (1 John 2:1 NASB)

The objection states that the phrase "if anyone sins, we have an Advocate with the Father" indicates that the Christians John addresses as "my little children" can and do sin, and they are forgiven because of their Advocate.

I contend that the "anyone" in the phrase is not a member of "my little children" and is not a Christian.

In order to interpret this verse, it's crucial to read the surrounding verses. As I noted in the previous objection analysis, the first chapter provides a gospel message, an explanation of how to gain fellowship with God and eternal life. This happens when a person confesses his sin (1 John 1:9) and is cleansed of all sin.

Therefore, in chapter two, when John says, "I am writing these things to you so that you may not sin," he is indicating that the message he has presented has this purpose. He has provided this gospel so that his readers will all receive and believe the transforming truth.

Responding to the gospel message makes people holy. It provides the means to stop sinning, because the blood of Jesus cleanses from all sin (chapter one verses seven and nine).

Does the blood of Jesus cleanse only some sin but not all? Of course not. It cleanses all sin, thereby making the believer holy and without sin. If professing believers actually do sin, that would mean that they did not heed the gospel message that John provided.

Here is where the confusion arises. John then gives us this very scenario. What happens if someone actually does sin?

It is essential for us to identify the people in mind, and the pronouns John uses help us understand his meaning. Most people paraphrase the verse in this fashion.

"John wrote this so that we wouldn't sin, but if we do sin, we have an Advocate with the Father, so we're forgiven."

Or, "This was written so that you won't sin, but

if you do, you're forgiven because of Jesus, your Advocate with the Father."

These are both inaccurate representations of what John is teaching. John gave them the message so that they would not sin, but if anyone does sin, that sinning person belongs to the group John described in chapter one, verse six—he is in darkness and in need of a savior.

The next point is critical. Notice the change in pronouns in the chapter two verse, "I am writing these things to *you* that *you* may not sin. And if *anyone* sins, *we* have and Advocate with the Father ..."

John changed from second person "you" to third person "anyone." The one who sins is not a member of the *you* group he addressed. When John wrote, "my little children, I am writing these things to *you* so that *you* may not sin," he then assumed that his readers had accepted this gospel and were now Christians. If he had meant the *anyone* to refer to his readers, it would have made more sense for him to say, "If any of *you* sins ..."

This is the reason he wrote that *we* have an Advocate instead of *he* (the anyone who sins) has an Advocate. The sinning person does not have an Advocate with the Father, because he is sinning and is an unbeliever. The Christians are the ones with the Advocate, and this Advocate can be shared with the sinning person.

This person who commits sin might be an unbelieving member of the church or one who has left the congregation. John was telling the Christians what to do in this situation.

This brings chapter one verse nine back into focus, part of the message that John gave to the readers. The Christians are supposed to share the gospel message of chapter one, the good news of their Advocate. They are to communicate this message to those who are sinning.

The news of the Advocate is to be shared with others, because he is the propitiation for the sins of the whole world, not just for the sins that John's readers committed in the past. The Christians had their sins forgiven already, but it was important for them to announce the availability of this forgiveness to *anyone* who sins. This *anyone* would not be part of the *we* who had already believed the message, but they would be considered part of the whole world, anyone who is not assumed to be a Christian.

Therefore, the possibility of a sinning Christian in "that you may not sin" is removed, because John has apparently placed *anyone* who actually does sin out of the addressed group by the use of the third-person pronoun.

The complete purpose of John's message is now clear. The first part of the purpose is to make sure that the people in the audience receive the gospel, become cleansed from all unrighteousness, and sin no more. The second part is to encourage them, once they are cleansed, to give the gospel message previously stated to anyone who sins.

This interpretation provides a more reasonable flow into verse three, an explanation of how to tell who are truly believers, by an examination of their actions.

> By this we know that we have come to know Him, if we keep His commandments. The one

who says, "I have come to know Him," and does not keep His commandments, is a liar, and the truth is not in him; but whoever keeps His word, in him the love of God has truly been perfected. By this we know that we are in Him: the one who says he abides in Him ought himself to walk in the same manner as He walked. (1 John 2:3-6 NASB)

By employing this test, the readers are able to identify who needs this message, and both purposes can be put into practice. They can share the great Advocate with the sinner so that he can be saved and stop sinning.

If actual Christians still sinned, then verses three through six wouldn't make sense. The standard for telling a Christian from a non-Christian is obedience, so if Christians sin, then those three verses would be false. Keeping God's commandments would not let us know if we have come to know Him.

The overwhelming testimony of the apostle John is that Christians are always obedient:

We know that no one who is born of God sins; but He who was born of God keeps him, and the evil one does not touch him. (1 John 5:18 NASB)

They are exactly like Jesus in their conduct, as the following verse states:

By this, love is perfected with us, so that we may have confidence in the day of judgment; because as He is, so also are we in this world. (1 John 4:17 NASB)

And everyone who has this hope fixed on Him purifies himself, just as He is pure. (1 John 3:3 NASB)

And those who sin are of the devil and in slavery:

He that committeth sin is of the devil, for the devil sinneth from the beginning, For this purpose the son of God was manifested, that he might destroy the works of the devil. (1 John 3:8 KJV)

Jesus answered them, "Truly, truly, I say to you, everyone who commits sin is the slave of sin." (John 8:34 NASB)

Readers should evaluate John's real message - I am writing these things to you so that you may not sin, and I hope you will accept it and carry this message to others, this message of the great Advocate who can cleanse anyone from all sin.

Objection #3 – Romans 7:14-25

One of the most common excuses for supposed sin in Christians comes from Romans chapter seven. Many interpret Paul's story of struggle with sin as one that occurred while he was a Christian, and if Paul struggled with sin, somehow that means that all Christians struggle in a similar way.

Yet, Paul was not describing his life as a regenerate man. He was describing his life under the Law, before Jesus stopped him during his murderous march toward Damascus.

How do we know Paul was unregenerate during

the time period he described? Up to this point, he had taken great pains to make these truths clear:

1. Christians have died with Christ. (Romans 6:3)
2. By doing this they have died to the Law. (Romans 7:6)
3. By this death they have also been freed from sin. (Romans 6:18, 22)
4. They have also become slaves of God and of obedience to God. (Romans 6:10-11, 13, 16, 22)

Yet, in Romans 7:14-25, Paul describes a different set of realities. He says that he is sold into bondage to sin instead of being freed from sin, which would be a contradiction if this section describes Paul's regenerated condition.

Also, later in Romans 8:9, Paul states, "However you are not in the flesh but in the Spirit, if indeed the Spirit of God dwells in you. But if anyone does not have the Spirit of Christ, he does not belong to Him." Yet, in Romans 7:14, Paul says that he is "of flesh." This is certainly not a description of one who is a Christian.

These two ideas, being of flesh and in slavery to sin, contradict the state of regenerated Christians that Paul taught in this section of Scripture.

Perhaps the most obvious contradiction occurs in Romans 7:23 where Paul says he is "a prisoner of the law of sin." Yet, in 8:2, he says that those who are in Christ Jesus have been set "free from the law of sin and of death."

Is a Christian a prisoner of the law of sin? Chapter eight says that he is not, but Paul says that he is such a prisoner in chapter seven. A Christian cannot be both a prisoner of sin and not a prisoner at the same time.

Therefore, Paul is not referring to himself in a regenerated state in the chapter seven passage.

Many claim that Paul's use of present tense in the chapter seven passage indicates that his description is his present condition.

First, a Greek tense does not necessarily indicate the time of an action. Paul sometimes uses present tense in an illustrative way, even when reflecting on a past event or series of events. We call this historical present.

Second, an appeal to the use of present tense cannot overcome the obvious contradictions between the condition of Paul in the chapter seven segment and the explicit descriptions of a Christian in the rest of the book

Third, those who insist that the present tense must mean that Paul is relating his present experience do not seem to realize that their assumption is self defeating.

For example, look at this verse:

> For what I am doing, I do not understand; for I am not practicing what I would like to do, but I am doing the very thing I hate. (Romans 7:15 NASB)

If this is Paul's present experience, then he does not understand what he is doing at the present time. What is he doing? Writing this verse. He does not even understand what he is writing, so he would be doing something incoherent—writing something that doesn't make sense to him.

Also, writing this verse isn't what he would like to do. In fact, he hates writing it, which means that he hates writing about truth. This is an absurdity. Therefore, this cannot be his present experience.

Here is another example:

> But if I do the very thing I do not want to do, I agree with the Law, confessing that the Law is good. So now, no longer am I the one doing it, but sin which dwells in me. (Romans 7:16-17 NASB)

If this is Paul's actual present experience, then his indwelling sin is writing this Scripture passage. So Paul not only doesn't understand what he is writing, his indwelling sin is actually writing it. If this is true, then how could we trust this passage? It would be incoherent, written by sin.

But those who claim that this is Paul's present experience would also claim that they don't think the present tense refers to what Paul is doing at the exact moment of writing the passage. They would claim that Paul is talking about recent events in his life.

If this is true, then Paul is actually talking about past events. Recent past is still past. Therefore, Paul is using illustrative present, not actual present, and appeal to present tense to prove Paul was talking about his current experience falls upon its own sword.

Therefore, this section of Romans chapter seven describes a man under the Law, before he becomes a Christian. So those who see parallels in their own lives are really finding evidence that they, themselves, are also unbelievers who need to cry out with Paul in his unregenerate state, "Wretched man that I am! Who will set me free from the body of this death?" and then find the power of God to be set free from sin.

Objection #4 – Hebrews 12

The following passage is often misused by Bible teachers in an attempt to show that all Christians sin.

> You have not yet resisted to the point of shedding blood in your striving against sin; and you have forgotten the exhortation which is addressed to you as sons, "My son, do not regard lightly the discipline of the Lord, nor faint when you are reproved by Him; For those who the Lord loves He disciplines, and He scourges every son whom He receives." It is for discipline that you endure; God deals with you as with sons; for what son is there whom his father does not discipline?
>
> But if you are without discipline, of which all have become partakers, then you are illegitimate children and not sons. Furthermore, we had earthly fathers to discipline us, and we respected them; shall we not much rather be subject to the Father of spirits, and live? For they disciplined us for a short time as seemed best to them, but He disciplines us for our good, that we may share His holiness. All discipline for the moment seems not to be joyful, but sorrowful; yet to those who have been trained by it, afterwards it yields the peaceful fruit of righteousness. (Hebrews 12:4-11 NASB)

These teachers explain that God disciplines us because of sins we commit, and since all true sons of God are disciplined, that must mean that all true Christians sin. Therefore, anyone who doesn't undergo this discipline due to their own sin must not be a true son and is unsaved.

As is the case with many false doctrines, the teachers fail to consider the passage in its larger context, and they bring a preconceived doctrine to the text, causing them to miss the real meaning.

Consider this sentence - "You have not yet resisted to the point of shedding blood in your striving against sin." (Verse four) The sin being strived against is not committed by the person being disciplined.

This is clear in the context. The writer has just finished a description of people who have been faithful, from Abel in chapter eleven, verse four, to, as the chapter ends, a list of those who suffered because of their faith.

> Others experienced mockings and scourgings, yes, also chains and imprisonment. They were stoned, they were sawn in two, they were tempted, they were put to death with the sword; they went about in sheepskins, in goatskins, being destitute, afflicted, ill-treated (men of whom the world was not worthy), wandering in deserts and mountains and caves and holes in the ground. (Hebrews 11:36-38 NASB)

In the chapter twelve passage, the writer is comparing his readers to those he wrote about earlier. His readers had not yet resisted sin to the point that these other people did, to the point of shedding blood. This sin is not their own sin; it is the sin of others, the sin of their persecutors.

The verse immediately preceding the chapter twelve section makes this obvious.

> For consider Him who has endured such hostility by sinners against Himself, so that you will not grow weary and lose heart. (Hebrews 12:3 NASB)

The writer is talking about the sin of the persecutors, not the sin of those being disciplined. Therefore, being disciplined as a son means that God is using persecutions to shape the son, to make him strong, to allow him to share in God's holiness.

It's important to understand that holiness is not merely sinlessness. It is being set apart for a purpose, to act according to all that God has in mind for us. We cannot complete that task until we are made ready for it, and our preparation includes suffering, often at the hands of sinners.

This happened even to Jesus.

> For it was fitting for Him, for whom are all things, and through whom are all things, in bringing many sons to glory, to perfect the author of their salvation through sufferings. (Hebrews 2:10 NASB)

> Although He was a Son, He learned obedience from the things which He suffered. And having been made perfect, He became to all those

who obey Him the source of eternal salvation (Hebrews 5:8-9 NASB)

Jesus endured this discipline, the sin that others brought against him. As verse three in chapter twelve says, we are to "consider him," the one who endured the sin of others. We are told to consider Jesus as an example, to endure as he endured, not regarding our own sin, but with reference to the sins of others.

The passage is meant to encourage obedient followers who are suffering at the hand of persecutors. It is telling them that faithful people have had it worse, and they made it through. There is a cloud of witnesses surrounding them (Hebrews 12:1) to counteract the sin that also surrounds. Follow in the footsteps of the forerunners, the enduring martyrs. Their light will guide the way.

Objection #5 – Galatians 2

Many assume from Galatians chapter two that the apostle Paul confronted the apostle Peter in Antioch regarding Peter's apparent lack of straightforwardness with the gospel. In this chapter, Paul equates this lack with dissembling, which some Bible versions translate as hypocrisy.

They conclude that since hypocrisy is sin, and since Peter committed hypocrisy, then Peter sinned under the new covenant. Therefore, since the great apostle sinned, it is reasonable to believe that other Christians sin, perhaps all of them.

It's no wonder so many people come to this faulty conclusion. The King James Version of the Bible gives strong evidence for their assumptions in Galatians 2:11-14.

> But when Peter was come to Antioch, I withstood him to the face, because he was to be blamed. For before that certain came from James, he did eat with the Gentiles: but when they were come, he withdrew and separated himself, fearing them which were of the circumcision. And the other Jews dissembled likewise with him; insomuch that Barnabas also was carried away with their dissimulation. But when I saw that they walked not uprightly according to the truth of the gospel, I said unto Peter before them all, If thou, being a Jew, livest after the manner of Gentiles, and not as do the Jews, why compellest thou the Gentiles to live as do the Jews?

Here is the same passage from the New American Standard Bible:

> But when Cephas came to Antioch, I opposed him to his face, because he stood condemned. For prior to the coming of certain men from James, he used to eat with the Gentiles; but when they came, he began to withdraw and hold himself aloof, fearing the party of the circumcision. The rest of the Jews joined him in hypocrisy, with the result that even Barnabas was carried away by their hypocrisy. But when I saw that they were not straightforward about the truth of the gospel, I said to Cephas in the

presence of all, "If you, being a Jew, live like the Gentiles and not like the Jews, how is it that you compel the Gentiles to live like Jews?"

The texts differ regarding the name of the person Paul confronted. Some Greek texts say that the man's name was Cephas, not Peter, and the translators of the NASB decided that these texts were more reliable. To many people, that difference poses no problem, because Peter was given the name Cephas by Jesus, as follows.

> He brought him to Jesus. Jesus looked at him and said, "You are Simon the son of John; you shall be called Cephas" (which is translated Peter). (John 1:42 NASB)

Besides this reference, the apostle Paul is the only person in Scripture to refer to the name Cephas using the Greek word for that name. One possible place is in Galatians chapter one, and there is variance in Greek texts in that passage as well.

Here is Galatians 1:18-19 in the King James Version:

> Then after three years I went up to Jerusalem to see Peter, and abode with him fifteen days. But other of the apostles saw I none, save James the Lord's brother.

And here it is in the New American Standard Bible

> Then three years later I went up to Jerusalem to become acquainted with Cephas, and stayed with him fifteen days. But I did not see any

other of the apostles except James, the Lord's brother.

In this passage, it is clear that Paul was referring to Peter, because he refers to him as an apostle in verse nineteen. That provides sufficient evidence that the KJV is correct in this case, and the name should be Peter.

Paul referred to Cephas using the Greek word for that name in other places:

> For I delivered to you as of first importance what I also received, that Christ died for our sins according to the Scriptures, and that He was buried, and that He was raised on the third day according to the Scriptures, and that He appeared to Cephas, then to the twelve. (1 Corinthians 15:3-5 NASB)

Paul differentiated between Cephas and the twelve. This isn't proof that Cephas was not part of the twelve, because Jesus easily could have appeared to one of the twelve and then to the twelve together, but the following use of Cephas casts doubt on that idea.

> Do we not have a right to take along a believing wife, even as the rest of the apostles and the brothers of the Lord and Cephas? (1 Corinthians 9:5 NASB)

Here Paul put Cephas outside of the group called "the apostles." It is theoretically possible that Paul could have listed Peter separately from "the apostles," but it would be unnatural to do so. It is more natural to assume that Paul was referring to a non-apostle.

We also have historical evidence pointing to the idea that Cephas in Galatians chapter two was not the apostle Peter. Eusebius wrote:

> And there is a story from Clement in the fifth of his Hypotyposeis in which he also says that Cephas, concerning whom Paul says: But, when Cephas came to Antioch, I resisted him to his face, was one of the seventy disciples, one who happened to have the same name as Peter the apostle. (Eusebius. The History of The Church. Book 1. 12)

This was Clement of Alexandria, who lived from about 150 AD to 215 AD and likely had access to information that we no longer have. Therefore, this is historical documentation indicating that this Cephas was not Peter. Cephas was one of the seventy disciples, though not one of the apostles.

Internal evidence in the Galatians chapter two passage also indicates that Cephas could not have been Peter. Note the verses leading up to Paul's opposition to Cephas.

> But on the contrary, seeing that I had been entrusted with the gospel to the uncircumcised, just as Peter had been to the circumcised (for He who effectually worked for Peter in his apostleship to the circumcised effectually worked for me also to the Gentiles), and recognizing the grace that had been given to me, James and Cephas and John, who were reputed

to be pillars, gave to me and Barnabas the right hand of fellowship, so that we might go to the Gentiles and they to the circumcised. (Galatians 2:7-9 NASB)

If Cephas were the same person as Peter, it wouldn't make sense for Paul to switch names in mid-sentence. Also, Peter himself used the Greek word for "Peter" in his own letters to Gentiles, so why would Paul use the Aramaic form (Cephas) to Gentiles, a form they would not be familiar with? That also wouldn't make sense.

The most reasonable conclusion is that Peter and Cephas were two different people.

We also have proof from the book of Acts that this person in Galatians two could not have been the apostle Peter:

> From there they sailed to Antioch, from which they had been commended to the grace of God for the work that they had accomplished. When they had arrived and gathered the church together, they began to report all things that God had done with them and how He had opened a door of faith to the Gentiles. And they spent a long time with the disciples.
>
> Some men came down from Judea and began teaching the brethren, "Unless you are circumcised according to the custom of Moses, you cannot be saved." And when Paul and Barnabas had great dissension and debate with them, the brethren determined that Paul and Barnabas and some others of them should go up to

Jerusalem to the apostles and elders concerning this issue. (Acts 14:26 - 15:2 NASB)

This Acts account perfectly fits the Galatians two account, and there is no other event recorded in Acts that coincides with Paul's account of a dispute in Antioch.

What did Paul and Barnabas do about the problem? They decided to consult the apostles and elders in Jerusalem. Who was one of those apostles? Peter himself:

> The apostles and the elders came together to look into this matter. After there had been much debate, Peter stood up and said to them, "Brethren, you know that in the early days God made a choice among you, that by my mouth the Gentiles would hear the word of the gospel and believe. And God, who knows the heart, testified to them giving them the Holy Spirit, just as He also did to us; and He made no distinction between us and them, cleansing their hearts by faith. Now therefore why do you put God to the test by placing upon the neck of the disciples a yoke which neither our fathers nor we have been able to bear? But we believe that we are saved through the grace of the Lord Jesus, in the same way as they also are." (Acts 15:6-11 NASB)

If Cephas in Galatians two really were Peter, it would make no sense for Paul to go all the way to Jerusalem to consult with the very person who was causing a problem. Peter was already in Jerusalem. He wasn't in Antioch. So it is impossible that Peter could have been the man Paul confronted in Galatians chapter two.

Another problem with believing that Peter was the one Paul criticized is that Peter would have gone against what he had so boldly stood for, that is, to show no partiality against the Gentiles. Throughout the book of Acts, Peter stood up for the Gentiles' reception of the gospel. Ever since his call by God to preach to Cornelius in Acts chapter ten, Peter was unwavering in his support of unfettered access to the gospel for the Gentiles. There is no evidence in Acts that Peter ever strayed from this steadfast support.

The evidence, both biblical and historical, is overwhelming that the man Paul confronted in Galatians was not the apostle Peter. That man was named Cephas, likely a Jew who sympathized with the "men from Judea."

Because of Peter's faithful defense of the Gentiles and their reception of the true gospel, we must not denigrate his legacy with the false charge that he was a hypocrite in Galatians chapter two. In addition, because this Cephas was not Peter, this passage provides no evidence for those who point to it as proof that Christians sin.

Also, since Paul's strong wording against Cephas indicates that his faith was in question (he stood condemned), charging Cephas with sin also in no way proves that Christians sin.

Objection #6 – The Epistles

One of the main arguments people make against

sinless Christianity relies on passages in the epistles to the churches. They claim that Paul and others refer to the letter recipients as saints, yet describe ongoing sin among these people. Therefore, this indicates the existence of sinning Christians.

If a writer labels readers as saints, it does not mean that every person who is referenced in the text is also a saint.

For example, in 2 Corinthians:

> Test yourselves to see if you are in the faith; examine yourselves! Or do you not recognize this about yourselves, that Jesus Christ is in you--unless indeed you fail the test? (2 Corinthians 13:5 NASB)

Paul refers to his audience as saints in the first chapter, but here in chapter thirteen, he tells the people to test themselves to see if they are in the faith. He wouldn't do that if he believed they were all, without exception, saints and true believers.

I am not going to analyze every letter that refers to saints and refute every perceived inference that these "saints" are sinning, but I will focus on the letter that is used most often to oppose sinless Christianity—the book of 1 Corinthians.

Consider this passage:

> And I, brethren, could not speak to you as to spiritual men, but as to men of flesh, as to babes in Christ. I gave you milk to drink, not solid food; for you were not yet able to receive it. Indeed, even now you are not yet able, for you are still fleshly. For since there is jealousy and

strife among you, are you not fleshly, and are you not walking like mere men? (1 Corinthians 3:1-3 NASB)

Many state that since these people are fleshly, the same people who are called saints in the epistle's greeting, then they are examples of sinful Christians.

In rebuttal, notice the "could not" in verse one. The past tense indicates that Paul was talking about a time in the past, probably the event mentioned in chapter two, verse one, "And when I came to you, brethren, I did not come with superiority of speech or of wisdom, proclaiming to you the testimony of God." This first meeting with the Corinthians was likely the time when Paul first introduced the Gospel to them.

Paul went on to explain that the "natural man" cannot understand God's wisdom, and he set this kind of man against one who has received the Spirit (2:11-14).

Therefore, in verse one of chapter three, Paul referred to his first presentation of the gospel to them and wrote that he could not speak to them at that time as to "spiritual men," those who had received the Spirit (2:12, 15), but as to "men of flesh," the "natural man" of 2:14. They could not have been saved at that time, because they had not yet heard the gospel.

"Men of flesh" is not descriptive of Christians, because the flesh has been crucified in a believer (Galatians 5:24). Therefore, when Paul wrote, "you are still fleshly," he meant that they were still not Christians. They were in the same state as they were when he first presented the gospel to them.

Yet, this conclusion does not mean that all of the addressed Corinthians were fleshly or unsaved, only those who were part of Paul's current focus in this section of the letter. Since Paul said that "there is jealousy and strife among" them, he was indicating that this was not true of everyone in the group. Only those who were guilty of the jealousy and strife would be considered fleshly by Paul, and those particular people were unsaved.

Some say that Paul's reference to the Corinthians in this section as "babes in Christ" means that they were baby Christians who needed to grow spiritually and mature. That is not the case. The Greek word for babes here is nepios, which has negative connotations.

Paul used the same word in 1 Corinthians 14:20 - "Brethren, do not be children in your thinking; yet in evil be babes, but in your thinking be mature."

He was not saying that he wanted them to be baby evil people who needed to grow and mature in evil. He wanted them to be removed from evil, separated from it, unfamiliar with it. In similar fashion, to be a babe in Christ means to be separated from and unfamiliar with Christ, not a baby Christian.

Therefore, the common notion that references to "saints" in epistle greetings must mean that all the readers are Christians is not supported by the text, and the resulting conclusion that Christians sin is also untrue.

If I were to examine every instance in which people infer from epistles that Christians in the church are sinning, I would point out similar problems with that interpretation. Churches have true believers as well as false converts, and the true believers are the ones who don't sin.

Objection #7 – The Lord's Prayer

Some people believe that since Jesus taught his disciples a prayer that included asking for forgiveness of sin, then all of his disciples must need forgiveness, which must mean that they all sin, including Christians in our current time.

This might be true if Jesus had been speaking to the same kind of followers that we are today. A disciple who followed Jesus before his death, burial, and resurrection and before the giving of the Holy Spirit was not the same as a disciple after these events.

The covenant changed, so it is reasonable to expect that important elements regarding our relationship with God changed as well. Commands that Jesus gave that were specific to the covenant his disciples were under at the time would not necessarily be in force under a new covenant.

For example, after Jesus healed a leper in Matthew 8:4, Jesus said, "See that you tell no one; but go, show yourself to the priest and present the offering that Moses commanded, as a testimony to them."

Since Jesus commanded the healed leper to do this, does that mean that all healed lepers in our time should present an offering that Moses commanded and show themselves to a priest? No. Jesus commanded the leper in this manner because he was still under the old covenant. New covenant believers are not to follow this command, because the situation has changed.

In a similar way, the disciples Jesus addressed when teaching them how to pray were under a covenant that could not cleanse them from sin. The new covenant changed that. Therefore, insisting that this prayer is a proof of ongoing sin in new covenant believers is invalid.

Also, would Jesus pray this prayer? If so, then it is possible for a sinless person to pray in this manner, and the claim that all who pray this prayer actually sin has no validity. On the other hand, if Jesus would not pray this prayer, then why should we? Under the new covenant, we are told to imitate Christ. Therefore, if Christ would not pray this way, then neither should we.

Again, the covenant has changed, and we are to live as Christ lived. In fact, the Bible says that we actually do live that way.

> By this, love is perfected with us, so that we may have confidence in the day of judgment; because as He is, so also are we in this world. (1 John 4:17 NASB)

In order to drive home the importance of this truth, let's examine the verse phrase by phrase:

By this - Refers to the previous phrase in verse sixteen: "God is love, and the one who abides in love abides in God, and God abides in him." The love that we have has its source in God.

Love is perfected with us - Jesus said that all the law and the prophets depend on loving God supremely and your neighbor as yourself. He also said that if we love him, we will keep his commandments. Since our love is perfected because of God's indwelling presence, that means that we are perfectly keeping his commandments.

So that we may have confidence in the day of judgment - Having perfect love and complete obedience gives us confidence, because God judges sinners, and we are no longer sinners. We are obedient. God does not condemn obedient people.

Because as He is, so also are we - How obedient are we? As Jesus is. This cannot allow for any sin at all.

In this world - This perfection of holiness doesn't wait for death or heaven. It is for the here and now, even in this corrupt, sin-sick world.

We really are like Jesus in this world—holy lights in whom love has been perfected. Let us believe this proclamation and live by it as confident followers of Christ who are no longer in bondage to sin.

Objection #8 – No One Else Believes This

Many people find comfort and security in numbers. They think that an idea has a firmer foundation if a majority, or at least a sizeable number, of people adhere to it.

That might be true in some categories of thought, but when it comes to eternal salvation, Jesus said:

> "Enter through the narrow gate; for the gate is wide and the way is broad that leads to destruction, and there are many who enter through it. For the gate is small and the way is narrow that leads to life, and there are few who find it." (Matthew 7:12-13 NASB)

We have proof from the mouth of the one who provides salvation that only a few will find it, that it is the minority, not the majority, who adhere to the truths that lead to eternal life.

Yet, some might still object that they don't know *anyone* who believes in this book's teachings. This isn't merely a few; it's practically no one.

It is possible that those who think this way have been insulated from the writings of those who do believe in sinless Christianity, especially those who wrote during the times of the early church.

Here are a few examples:

> And let those who are not found living as He taught, be understood to be no Christians, even though they profess with the lip the precepts of Christ; for not those who make profession, but those who do the works, shall be saved. - Justin Martyr

> But the One who raised Christ from the dead will raise us also, if we do his will, walk in his commandments, love what he loved, and keep ourselves from all unrighteousness, greed, love of money, evil speaking, and lies. - Polycarp

> But when they should be converted and come to repentance, and cease from evil, they should have power to become the sons of God, and to receive the inheritance of immortality which is given by Him. - Irenaeus

As quoted earlier, John Wesley, from a more modern time, agreed:

A Christian is so far perfect as not to commit sin. This is the glorious privilege of every Christian, yes, though he be but a babe in Christ.

Therefore, there are others who believe this truth. The problem is that these voices have been silenced in the modern church, making the path to eternal life even narrower.

It's time to restore these voices, to shout the true gospel from the rooftops, that Jesus can and does cleanse his followers from all unrighteousness, that we can be set free from the shackles of sin to love and serve him with all our hearts.

Conclusion

The church of today has raised many other objections to these biblical doctrines, too many to list and refute in this small book. Yet, I would respond to them in ways resembling my other responses in this appendix.

The two most common categories of objections:

1. Examples of believers under the old covenant who sin—King David, Moses, Solomon, etc. Since they are all under the old covenant, which could make no one perfect, using such examples in order to prove the nature of a new covenant believer is invalid.

2. Examples of sinning "believers" under the new covenant—members of the Galatian and Corinthian churches, etc. The New Testament provides examples of sinners within the body

of Christ, but that does not mean that these people are truly born again. In many of the places where epistle writers mention the sinners among them, they also provide statements that these people are not true Christians, and their sinning behavior proves their unsaved status.

The bottom line is that there is nothing in the Bible that definitively states that Christians sin after their regeneration, while there are several straightforward and clear statements that they no longer sin, that they are wholeheartedly obedient to God.

It is difficult to guess the motivations of those who argue against God's power to make his followers holy, who try to prove that sin is essential or inevitable, who claim that those who profess to live a holy life are liars. Perhaps they feel justified by the fact that they are supported by the vast majority in the church, and they want to silence dissenters. Perhaps they have been deceived by centuries of anti-holiness teaching that is pervasive in the church today. Perhaps they feel trapped by sin and they see no way to escape from its chains.

Because of their bodily urges and their slavery to their fleshly desires, they can't imagine being without sin until they die and are set free from their earthly form. Yet, if they believe that death is the only way to be truly freed from sin, that Jesus cannot provide that freedom while they live here on earth, they must by necessity believe that death is more powerful than the Lord. Death is able to automatically provide freedom from sin while the Lord could not.

Therefore, for them, death is their savior from sin, not Jesus Christ.

May it never be!

Jesus is far and away more powerful than sin and death. He is the only one who can set a prisoner free from both dominions. To assume otherwise will keep prisoners in chains forever, in this world and in the world to come.

The common thread in all of these objections to sinless Christianity is deception. Whether by majority opinion, by teachers, or by sin itself, the objectors are deceived. They are imprisoned by one of Satan's tactics—to make people think they are among the saved when in reality they are not, and they will be condemned as a result.

Yet, there is a solution, a way of escape for all who, for one reason or another, have not yet come to believe the true gospel. The Bible describes this freedom again and again, that God is powerful enough and loves you enough to set you free.

If you are unconvinced, I urge you to read through these proofs once more and ask God to show you whether or not he can break the chains of sin and set you free. When you decide to believe in that benevolent power, then you can and will be free indeed.